WHO AM I TO LEAD?

THE WORLD IS WAITING FOR YOU

TORIN PEREZ

Dedicated to TJ and my future children

CONTENTS

YOUR IMPACT

INTRODUCTION

In the fall of 2016, I was in Boston, Massachusetts, visiting one of my best friends when I wrote the first version of *Choosing the Glass Half Full*, the first essay in this book. The writing came over me like a flood, hours after a conversation we had about our aspirations in life. Little did I know that that moment was the beginning of a new journey for me. I never could have predicted that over the next year I would have conversations with dozens of people during my travels, trying to better understand what stories and lessons would resonate deepest with readers interested in their leadership and personal development.

Through conversations on airplanes, at bars, and in workplaces across the country, I gained an appreciation and awareness of the issues many people are grappling with in their lives—topics that each deserve their own essay, as you may have already seen in the table of contents. Ultimately, this book is for anyone who wants to live more fully, find meaningful work, and learn how they can grow as leaders both personally and professionally, no matter where they are in their careers.

I set out to write concise, bite-sized essays that can be read in a few minutes so that readers can get the quick hits of inspiration and insights they need in minimal time. As you are reading this book, you can jump around to different essays that sound interesting or open the book to any essay and get started. I hope that *Who Am I to Lead?* will be a steady companion with you on your journey to becoming the leader you are meant to be.

Are you ready to get started? The world is waiting for you.

YOUR MINDSET

CHOOSING THE GLASS HALF FULL

I believe this world can be viewed in one of two ways: glass half full or glass half empty. This is an old but simple analogy for understanding how we view our lives, possibilities, and how we interpret events. How you view your glass influences what you think you can do, and the subsequent actions you take. The person who believes the glass is half full believes there is enough good fortune to go around. They are more generous with others because they live with an abundance mindset. The person who believes the glass is half empty believes there is little if anything to be shared. This person lives in a space of scarcity and perceives limited resources. Which view do you most frequently identify with?

At every stage of achievement and accomplishment, think about how your perspective on life influences how you interpret things. Let's say you were accepted to Harvard University and decide to attend. That's a pretty fantastic accomplishment. When you arrive on campus, you enjoy the initial rush of excitement of now being a Harvard student, but as the honeymoon phase ends, you begin thinking about all of the other students who have come before you and the students who are now getting better grades than you. You may perceive that you are getting left behind, falling out of contention for the best internships, and consequently that you won't get a great job like most Harvard students. Which outlook do you think this is?

It's glass half empty because you have forgotten that you are attending one of the most prestigious colleges in the world. Carrying around this mindset will impact how you interact with your classmates. You might be less willing to offer your help. It will also impact how you feel about yourself, perhaps leading you to constantly search for validation in ranking yourself against others, which is a never ending and fruitless battle. You might start focusing on the paths of others instead of your own.

What separates some of the best athletes and champions from the rest is their focus on being at their best—not beating someone else's best. They are fueled to reach their own maximum potential, something that you can only see if you are looking reflectively and consciously at yourself, not others. We each have in us the potential to discover our purpose in life and in our careers, but we cannot realize our potential with a glass-half-empty mentality. When we, as individuals, open up to the possibility of seeing the glass half full, we open the doors to the potential that awaits us.

Whenever I ask people if they would rather be rich and unhappy or poor and happy, they always pick the latter. Asking that question gets us to think about what's really important because most of us are blindly seeking riches. Our happiness is important because it affects our wellbeing and the people around us at home and at work.

I've found that having an optimistic view of the world has allowed me to experience joy and gratitude on a daily basis. I'm constantly inspired because the optimist in me sees the potential in every opportunity. The optimist in me imagines that as you read this you are thinking about your own ability to positively change the way you think and approach life. I believe that the ingenuity, spirit, and passion that resides in you is just waiting to be unleashed.

The good news is that if you primarily have a glass half empty, pessimistic view of the world, it's possible to change. I believe what I'm about to share about with you just may inspire you to do so.

In 2015, *Fortune* recognized my mentor, Frances Hesselbein, as one of the world's fifty greatest leaders, and in 2016 the American Foundation for Age Research recognized her for her lifetime achievements. While Frances has been admired for a long time for her many achievements, it's her positive approach to life that has invigorated her with vitality every step of the way. In 1990, she left the helm of the Girl Scouts of the USA after thirteen successful years as CEO to start a leadership institute with the late Peter Drucker. The institute is still thriving today under France's leadership as the *Frances Hesselbein Leadership Forum*. When people ask why she remains hopeful about the future, she often jokes that even her blood type is B-positive! She has proven that age is irrelevant and it's what you do with your life that matters. She wakes up every day inspired and travels to her office four days each week.

Frances proves that there is no limit to what we can contribute to the world when we start looking at the glass half full. Our abilities are not stagnant or inert. They are fluid, constantly growing, morphing, and being molded by our experiences and education. We are all capable of seeing the glass half full because there is an abundance to be shared, given, and kept for ourselves.

Looking at the glass half full doesn't mean ignore the news and the serious crises that may be plaguing your community and communities around the world. That would lead to naïve and blind optimism. What I am encouraging you to do is take on a new attitude that will allow you to reach for your highest potential, share in the journey with others, and discover the inspiring stories of people who are contributing to the world in positive ways. Who knows, one day it might be your story that may inspire someone to choose the glass half full, all because you offered them a glimmer of hope.

THE THERMOMETER
VS.
THE THERMOSTAT

Think of the last time a stranger smiled at you, or the last time you smiled at a stranger. I imagine that the smile was reciprocated, or if not, there was an awkward avoidance of further eye contact. The person who smiled was at the beginning of a ripple effect, prompting the person they smiled at to respond. Have you ever been in the presence of someone with an infectious laugh or someone who is carefree on the dance floor? That person's behavior probably encouraged you to laugh and maybe even dance! In a figurative sense, that person acted like a thermostat in that situation. Unlike a thermometer, which only takes the temperature of a room and simply displays that temperature, a thermostat can adjust and change the temperature of a room. The thermostat is a tool always available to us.

Gina, one of my friends and former colleagues from the volunteer Junior Board of Harlem Educational Activities Fund in New York City was struggling to communicate effectively with her boss. She had become very unhappy in her role even though she felt deeply aligned with the mission of the organization she was working for. She did not feel confident about the conversation she needed to have with her boss regarding her role and responsibilities and a review of a project she was leading. She was frustrated because she felt she was not being recognized for her contributions and feared that her boss was unable to see her potential. This was making her lose confidence even though she felt that she was doing well. It's easy to identify with how she felt. When we lack confidence, it's difficult to go out and do our best and be our best. It's easy to shy away from the conversation and the challenge to make things right.

At times in the workplace we may have to deal with varying degrees of bureaucracy and politics. Sometimes we need to have difficult conversations. We may be hesitant to engage with a boss, cautious of what emotions they may evoke in us based on our past experiences. I was happy when Gina shared what she was going through, and I shared this analogy with her: acting like a thermostat is a choice and a mindset. Gina is talented, passionate, and dedicated to her work. I reassured her that that is how many of our colleagues felt about her. I also explained to her how the thermometer would take the situation as it is, while the thermostat would go into the office and set a new temperature. In our conversation, she decided to start shifting her internal thoughts to focus on what she wants and how she would like to show up differently going forward. She visualized her excitement and honesty, opening the doors to more frequent and constructive communication with her boss. In the following days, she showed up, proactively scheduled a meeting with her boss, and proceeded to transform the relationship. She's since learned from the lesson of this experience and continues to reap its benefits.

In another situation, I was speaking to new college scholars and their mentors at America Needs You, an organization that fights for the economic mobility of ambitious, first-generation college students. While I was meditating before the session, I decided that I would be the thermostat in the room that day. During our session, I prompted the young people in attendance to celebrate each other with applause, and asked them to practice their dance moves as a symbol of their dance with adversity. At the end, one young man stood up to speak in front of the group. It was his first time speaking in front of such a large audience. He thanked the speakers of the day and shared a short story about his unlikely journey to become the first in his family to go to college. As his eyes welled up with tears, there was an emotional shift in the audience and many of his peers became teary eyed too. He unconsciously became a thermostat in that moment, transforming the experience of dozens of people who may have also been thinking of standing to speak and didn't. Thanks to his courage, several other students stood up to speak too because he changed the temperature in the room.

Choosing to be a thermostat can make a big difference.

DEFEATING IMPOSTOR SYNDROME

Impostor Phenomenon is a term that was coined in 1978 by clinical psychologists Pauline R. Clance and Suzanne A. Imes. In their paper titled *"The Imposter Phenomenon in High Achieving Women: Dynamics and Therapeutic Intervention,"* they state that, "despite their earned degrees, scholastic honors, high achievement on standardized tests, praise and professional recognition from colleagues and respected authorities, [the high achieving women surveyed] do not experience an internal sense of success. They consider themselves to be 'impostors.' Women who experience the impostor phenomenon maintain a strong belief that they are not intelligent; in fact they are convinced that they have fooled anyone who thinks otherwise." While this research focused on women, we know now that both men and women are affected by this phenomenon, also known as impostor syndrome.

I've met many high-achievers who have received an award or opportunity they think they do not deserve. The thing is that as human beings we all have moments when we experience the fear that we are not good enough. Although our list of accomplishments and accolades may be long, all of us at any point in our lives and careers are susceptible to this feeling and ask ourselves questions like, "Am I supposed to be here?"

I think about when I got the chance to go to Lafayette College on a full-tuition scholarship from the Posse Foundation, an organization that identifies public high school students with extraordinary academic and leadership potential who may be overlooked by traditional college selection processes. The second I laid my head down in bed those first few nights on campus and heard insects loudly chirping outside, I realized how out of place I felt. I had come from an inner city neighborhood of Brooklyn and hearing wildlife, even just insects, was a big change from the bustle of car horns and concrete city life.

I also felt out of place because most of the students were of a different socio-economic status than me; they were mostly upper middle class and affluent whites. I thought about how I would fit in. At times I found myself embellishing stories about the tough inner city to confirm the ideas and assumptions that some of my classmates already had of Brooklyn. It was uncomfortable yet it gave me a sense of identity in a foreign place.

Things didn't really make sense until I was selected for the WorldTeach program, which provides volunteer teachers to meet local needs and promote responsible global citizenship in developing countries. I went to South Africa for the summer after my freshman year. Being so far away from home and everything I was familiar with helped me to find myself. Living with a German host family, working with teenage entrepreneurs in a black township, and teaching English in a colored community revealed to me how I could feel connected to each of these groups of people. I didn't see them as different. I viewed them as human like me, in different places, affected by different conditions. That summer changed my life forever. I left the African continent inspired with possibilities for the impact that I could make in this world and how far and how high I could reach for my potential.

Fascinated by the differences in socio-economic status between each of the communities I was exposed to, I was inspired to learn more about business and economics. My freshman year of college I was in the biology major track, which meant the following summer I had to convince a business corporation to hire a biology student fresh off of a teaching experience for a summer internship. Looking back now, I see that that was when I first learned the power of passion and storytelling. Several companies turned me down, but once I got that first phone interview with Bloomberg LP, I knew what I wanted to say and I knew I wanted that internship more than anything else. The people whose lives I would touch in the future depended on it.

In the summer of 2007, I landed my first corporate internship at Bloomberg and impostor syndrome raised its ugly head again. There I was at a prestigious company I had not previously heard of, and the vast majority of interns and employees I could see were white. So that feeling of impostor syndrome turned into a need to prove myself, but the extra motivation I put in actually revealed my potential that summer. I ended up being a critical part of my intern team, which competed in an internal company stock competition. We finished in second place, just behind a team that had one of the interns' stock-trader parents advising them. That chip on my shoulder led Trevor Fellows, the Global Head of Media Sales, to say that I was, perhaps, the best intern he ever had on his team. And that affirmation was just what I needed at that stage in my life to stop myself from feeling defeated before the game had even begun.

Personal development icon Jim Rohn teaches this lesson: beware of the thief in the streets who's after your purse, but be even more aware of the thief in your mind who's after your promise.

Impostor syndrome is that thief.

You must know that you are not alone in fighting this deeply human challenge to believe in yourself enough to do what you feel you were put on this planet to do. Whether it's to become a musician, a world-class entrepreneur, a CEO, or President of the United States, listen to the truth within yourself. Know that opportunities are presented because you deserve them. If you don't receive it at this moment, that could just be an indication that it may not be the right time yet, or the right opportunity. Life is a journey of opening and closing doors. Be sure to open the door to the truth of your promise. By living your truth, you will be set free to be everything you imagine in this world.

OUR SMARTPHONE ADDICTION

With the advent of smartphones, social media platforms have become fixtures in our lives. Over 2 billion people have accounts on Facebook, and hundreds of millions more are active users on many other popular platforms. For networking professionals, LinkedIn is available to discover new career opportunities. Pinterest and Instagram provide outlets for photographers, artists, and creatives to share their work. For people who want to say something succinctly, Twitter is a place to share perspectives and join conversations with others through hashtags. For people of any age and from every continent in the world, Facebook is a way to reconnect with old friends and find new ones.

Each of these platforms understands that they must innovate and create new features in order to remain relevant to their users. There is big money in big data and advertising, so each platform also understands that more active users scrolling, clicking, watching, and sharing means more opportunities to use that data for greater revenues.

While smartphone apps can be powerful tools for many important daily tasks, including GPS, staying organized, and reading and sending emails, the incessant use of our phones encourages addictive behaviors. Tap, type, swipe, and click. Pings, rings, texts and alerts. These engagements with our phones are actually delivering quick hits of a chemical in our bodies called dopamine, which is highly addictive. Dopamine is activated when we check something off of our to-do list, or when we go to check the notifications in our phones. When there is too much dopamine in our bodies, another chemical called cortisol activates and begins to break down our immune system, which protects us from getting sick.

Even knowing the risks, I have found it difficult at times to use social media in moderation. When I am not sharing posts, I am still scrolling, reading, watching, and liking. At times, I feel tired and depleted from checking my phone too much. I find myself getting upset during meals with friends and family members who can't leave their phones off the table or put their phones on silent during our time together. I started thinking about what I could do differently and how people could live healthier lives in the age of social media and smartphones.

First, I have had to acknowledge that this is part of the current reality we are living in, a time when we have access to mini-computers in our pockets. These powerful devices at our fingertips, which allow us to get information, exchange information, stay connected, and even do business simultaneously and instantaneously, have become critical to our livelihoods. It's hard to disconnect from something that is integrally woven into our daily habits, processes, and lives.

Second, I've thought about what our phone addictions might be costing us in our interpersonal relationships. I've seen friends get anxious to check their phones when they see someone else on their phone. I've stressed to people why I do everything I can to not have my phone visible or on sound when we're having a meal.

Looking at or engaging with your phone while you're with somebody else is a visible cue that signals to the other person that they are not as important as whoever is texting, liking, or sharing on your phone. It's not uncommon to see people sitting at a table with each other in silence because they are all on their phones. Or maybe they're engaging with people online who are commenting on the picture they posted of the food they are eating at that very moment—instead of engaging with the people they're actually eating with. It's easy to see how using our phones this way can erode the quality of our relationships because we aren't giving or getting someone's undivided attention.

Third, I've observed my own patterns and have sought ways to do things differently. Here are some tips that have worked for me:

1. Decide to check social media only at certain times of day, for a specific amount of time. This will immediately limit how long and how frequently you check. Make this non-negotiable.
2. Put your phone on silent and practice giving your undivided attention to anyone you may be having a conversation with, whether it's in passing, at meetings in your office, at lunch with colleagues, or at dinner with friends and family.
3. Turn off visible notifications and alerts on your social media as they will be useless until #1.
4. Get accustomed to feeling at ease when your phone is put away on silent or on airplane mode. Not everything is an emergency. Not all notifications must be checked immediately. Separation anxiety from our phones doesn't have to be a thing.

Let your presence be a gift. Let your phone be a tool you use when you choose.

TRUSTING DESTINY

I've come to truly appreciate the connectedness of life's adventure. So much so, that I look forward to discovering the good fortune that awaits at every corner and the providential moments that make me look up to heaven with gratitude. I want to draw your attention to how destiny has played a role in my life, with the hope that you too will devote some time to introspection and see the myriad ways destiny has also played out in your life.

I truly believe nothing happens on our time. Rather, God, who people of varying faiths may call different things, is the master coordinator, mapping out our paths in this great adventure we call life. There is a saying that goes, "If you want to make God laugh, tell him your plans." It's hard sometimes to see the events and circumstances that befall us as God's plan because we sometimes disconnect from our faith, thinking it's our hard work and dedication alone that are reaping the results we desire: the promotion, the new home, acceptance to the school of our choice, and on and on. I believe that destiny is God's divine plan for each of us, and I believe that trusting that plan has prepared me for some of the biggest moments and opportunities in my life.

When I was a sophomore in high school, I was captain of my junior varsity basketball team. The one game of the season that the varsity coach came to see me play, I scored a bunch of points including an epic fourth quarter back and forth against a childhood rival, where my team came out on top in the final seconds of the game. The impression I made on the coach during that game is what helped me to become one of the few junior varsity players to make the cut for the varsity team the following year.

I played for the varsity team for two years. After a disappointing first year where we underperformed for the level of talent we had, I looked forward to my senior year and hoped to finish my high school career on a strong note. I had a great showing at a few basketball camps the summer after junior year and had garnered some attention from a few Division 2 and Division 3 college programs. It was looking like I would pursue a college basketball career until destiny revealed the true plan ahead.

Unbeknownst to me, during my junior year, a few outstanding students became the first Posse Scholars from my high school. Whether it was my good standing with our college counselor or just a good reputation in general at my school, the recipients decided to recommend me as a potential candidate for the Posse Scholars, which included a full-tuition scholarship to one of America's best colleges and universities. When I first heard about it I was blown away, and thinking about it now still gives me butterflies. During the fall of my senior year, I went through the three-part interview process for the program, gaining more confidence after each interview and believing that somehow this opportunity presented itself just for me. The thing was, if I got in, there would be a required 8-month pre-collegiate training program to get prepared for the academic rigors and new environment I would be entering. This meant I would miss several games and that my senior year basketball campaign would essentially be over.

Well, as it turned out, Lafayette College selected me for the Posse Scholarship, and they also had a Division 1 basketball team. Once I got the scholarship, I inquired about playing basketball at Lafayette, but the program relied heavily on recruiting talent as opposed to taking walk-ons. I decided to get into the best shape of my life, work on my game, and try out for Lafayette's team.

Little did I know that the pre-collegiate training program was preparing me for what was to come next. College opened my eyes to how I could lead important dialogues on campus and serve in leadership roles in campus organizations. When I got to Lafayette, it was these kinds of opportunities that I fell in love with, while simultaneously falling out of love with playing basketball. While I did play intramural basketball for fun, I knew I wouldn't pursue my childhood dreams seriously ever again, and instead, I embraced life as a leader at my school.

I held leadership roles in two campus organizations that won honors for making exemplary contributions to the campus community. While serving as a resident advisor, my staff team was recognized with Staff of the Year honors. That year on staff I helped make the emergency call to get help for an unresponsive resident. I also volunteered as a career services ambassador to promote opportunities for students to develop their resumes and skills and find internships.

Had I not been recognized as a candidate for Posse, I may have decided to pursue basketball at a different college. Without the Posse scholarship, I would have likely attended a less reputable school with fewer opportunities. Without exposure to all of the leadership activities and unique opportunities at Lafayette, I may not have developed into the person I am today.

As we go through life, we will never be able to foresee everything. What we can do is start paying more attention to what we can see in the moment. As you will read in my essay on serendipity, there are things that happen to us that are completely unpredictable, yet fortuitous in their own ways. I've grown to have such a trust in destiny, and it's largely because of a few key beliefs that I want to share with you here:

1. You won't be presented with an opportunity that you are not ready for. Instead of being overwhelmed, I feel excited for each opportunity that comes my way because of this belief. In *Defeating Impostor Syndrome*, I highlight how even the highest achievers don't believe they deserve certain opportunities. It's important not to think or talk yourself out of something before you get started.
2. Do the work, don't stop pushing, and trust that the timing will be just right. Some of my friends jokingly say that my nickname is "Stay Ready" because they have seen me pull out a crisp business card for a stranger on a weekend after a brief elevator conversation. Some of those connections have opened doors. One gentleman I met in an elevator was a senior leader at a world-renowned media company. He was dressed in a t-shirt and jeans at the time we met. The next time we met several months later, he was dressed in a suit and sitting in his NYC skyscraper corner office, inquiring about my interest in joining his organization. You cannot predict who the strangers you meet will turn out to be, but you can commit to continually improving yourself and putting in the work to be ready for moments like this.

3. Know that you were put on this planet for a reason, and while you may think that reason is a destination, it's actually a destiny. If we pigeonhole our lives into a particular goal or dream job, that's just a destination. With destiny, the future is an open book of possibilities to take on different roles and make contributions personally, professionally, and to your community at different stages of your life.

We never know how the mystery of destiny will develop before our eyes. One thing we can do is open our eyes to the possibilities.

SETTING AND RISING TO EXPECTATIONS

On the path to achieving great success in life, I believe we must have high expectations for ourselves and an even higher appreciation for the journey. To give you a little more context around what I mean, let me take you back to some of my earliest encounters with high expectations.

In the summer of 1993, my dad brought me to Queens, New York, to join the Impact Youth Basketball League, a program to introduce youths, ages four to seventeen years old, to playing basketball in an organized environment. An impressionable young boy, just five years old at the time, I liked the motto of the Impact League: *Make an impact in life, excel in school*. Growing up with two immigrant parents, it was no secret that they thought education was one of the keys to my future. I didn't really need that reminder from Impact, but the motto was a powerful statement about the program.

The motto demonstrated that Coach Ken Vickers, who founded the program, cared about the children beyond the basketball court. Basketball was a tool for lessons in character and virtues like focus, discipline, and commitment to practice and hard work. If any of us wanted to be like Mike (Michael Jordan, that is), Coach Ken wanted us to know we would have to first do well enough academically in school to be able to get into college and meet GPA eligibility requirements for a NCAA team. The summer program was a great display of positive work in the Queens community, providing an outlet for children and teens to play basketball in a constructive learning environment instead of being inactive and idling away their time.

While at Impact, I was one of just a few players chosen for the select team. We traveled to different cities and states competing in tournaments against other top teams. We even won a tournament at the famous Gaucho Gym in the Bronx, New York. Coach expected us to believe in ourselves enough so that we could go out and win, no matter the competition. We often rose to those expectations as a team. When coaches and mentors have high expectations for your success, when they see more for you than you may see for yourself—that is an amazing gift. I still have all of the trophies that we won during those days, and they remind me of the excellence and success we were able to build towards year after year.

As a member of the Junior Board of Directors at HEAF from 2014 to 2017, I saw how much of a difference it makes for youths to have resources, support, and high expectations. One of HEAF's programs is actually called High Expectations Middle School Enrichment. HEAF has led underserved students in Harlem on their journeys through middle school, high school, and college since 1989. As part of the program, students come in during middle school to receive academic and social-emotional support and get introduced to the HEAF motto: *Where college is the rule*. It's no wonder these students, and students like those selected to be Posse Scholars, go on to far exceed the national graduation rate of 59 percent. As of 2017, HEAF students had a 100 percent graduation rate from high school and an 83 percent graduation rate from college within four to six years. At Posse, groups of inner-city students, typically ten per cohort, graduate from the nation's most prestigious colleges at 90 percent. Because the power of high expectations positively influenced me throughout my youth and college, I know how valuable it can be to have people encouraging you to become the best you can be.

Now in my professional work in leadership development, I've learned that there's another story about expectations that isn't often talked about. Impostor syndrome is a common challenge we face as high achievers—wondering whether we belong on the bigger and bigger stages we progress to. As our roles and titles get bigger, and as our responsibilities grow, people begin to expect more from us. Not graduating on time, failing to get into the best college, or simply disappointing your teachers and parents is one thing. But when expectations are not met in work settings, it can cost you your job, and your company stands to lose a lot too. The stakes are much higher. I meet people who are fatigued and frustrated because of the weight and pressure of these expectations. Work and dream jobs can become a nightmare of daily stress if you aren't careful.

I'll always remember this quote from Tony Robbins: "Success without fulfillment is the ultimate failure." As we continue on the path of achievement and get selected for bigger opportunities, we must never forget this. It's possible to be at the pinnacle of perceived success, while being completely miserable inside. This is not the way to live. Sometimes we need to pause and do one simple thing—consciously appreciate where we are in life.

When I've been invited to facilitate programs and speak at prestigious institutions, I've found it easy to get overwhelmed with the rising expectations of new levels of achievement. To combat this, I make it a point to appreciate everything, even the small stuff. Some people keep a journal and write down things they are grateful for each day. Some people take some quiet time each day to meditate and express gratitude. Personally, I choose to enjoy moments of gratitude as frequently as I can, sometimes multiple times a day.

When I feel the heaviness of expectations, it's a trigger for me to consciously think about and feel the gratitude for the opportunity. To give a TED Talk and speak about an idea worth spreading—that can be a scary stage to stand on. At the same time, you have the opportunity to share an idea that you created and add value to people's lives. That deserves real appreciation. Thinking about all of the work that has gone into building my business, I'm so grateful for the challenges that make me a better businessperson. I look forward to serving more people, and I'm appreciative of the opportunity to do so.

As the stakes get higher and expectations rise, so too must our appreciation for the path that's been paved for us to walk.

SERENDIPITY

Some call it luck. Some call it providence. Some call it serendipity. There definitely is something to being in the right place, at the right time, with the right person, having the right conversation. Somehow everything aligns, the moment happens, and doors open to fortuitous things. It's a beautiful experience to have once in a while, but I have made a habit of it. I experience serendipitous events frequently. We tend to see serendipity when we are open to it. Serendipity is not something we can embrace, but rather something we welcome into our lives.

I show up with a conscious appreciation for the present moment, and in that moment, I am appreciative of the person who is with me. I am appreciative of their presence, words, actions, and conversation. Most of the time, if it is a casual conversation with no agenda identified beyond getting to know one another, it's the freedom to explore, discover, and listen to their story that intrigues me to be open to all topics and directions the conversation may go. This has served me well as I have often felt deep emotions and even cried with new acquaintances. For the most part, I have developed long-lasting relationships with people even after only spending a short time together.

Let me share a series of serendipitous events that have happened for me. One of those stories is about my dear friend Yasmine El-Baggari. We are both StartingBloc Social Innovation Fellows and one of our mutual friends told each of us that we should meet each other. I was excited to hear her story as our friend had shared wonderful things about her and what she was up to in her life.

When we got together to meet for the first time in April 2015, we talked for four hours. Many tears were shed and personal stories exchanged. Part of the serendipity was that this exchange even came to be. It was a coincidence that we had a mutual friend who held both of us in high esteem. It just so happened that he was thoughtful enough to see the potential friendship waiting to blossom. During my conversation with Yasmine, I came to understand how a young woman in her early twenties saw the world and had created opportunities, seemingly out of thin air, to sit in important rooms with high-level people. The serendipity of our meeting was uncanny because it was not only the right timing to become friends, but also the right timing to find synergy in our work.

In August 2015, I went to San Diego, California, to join Yasmine in an incredible initiative that brought young African leaders from over twenty countries to the United States for a series of leadership development programs. In September 2015, I did a homestay with her family in Rabat, Morocco, while attending Shape Africa, the Global Shapers of the World Economic Forum conference, and giving a keynote talk. Based on her recommendation, I also applied to One Young World. In November 2015, I attended the conference in Bangkok, Thailand, where I joined young leaders from 196 countries to build connections and solutions towards the United Nations' Global Goals. In December 2015, also based on her recommendation, I invested in attending *Date With Destiny*, a signature six-day program with Tony Robbins in Boca Raton, Florida. It was a whirlwind of a year, but it was one of the best years of my life!

Each of these experiences were incredible in their own way, and they may not have happened if it were not for an introduction, a great conversation, and the willingness to be open to what serendipity had in store. Sitting at a dinner table with a brand new acquaintance, I committed to going on these four adventures, without any advance knowledge of how I would make it all happen.

In Morocco, the audience I had a chance to speak to came from fifty countries, so I couldn't miss the opportunity to inspire such a diverse audience. For One Young World, I had to run a successful crowdfunding campaign to get there. More than seventy people contributed to my $5,000 campaign, which covered airfare and conference attendee expenses. Dozens of people provided small amounts of money, but the contributions added up, and my backers' positive words and encouragement were inspiring. My path to getting to One Young World also inspired many of the people who were there, especially the corporate professionals whose employers fully sponsored their attendance. At *Date With Destiny*, I experienced 12+ hour days with Tony Robbins; a deep and transformative dive that has provided me with a distinct clarity around my life and what I hope to give while I make my mark. I met wonderful human beings at the event, and I stepped away from it with the feeling that there would be nothing to ever get in my way again. Fast forward to today, I'm still fired up, confident, excited, and beaming with light and encouragement and working to help others find and pursue their paths with passion and faith.

All of these events happened because of that fateful meeting with Yasmine in April of 2015, and amazingly, there's still more to this story. When I applied to the inaugural TED Residency early in 2016, I had to provide three references. One came from Yasmine and one came from a senior level executive that I met at One Young World. Talk about serendipity. Two of my three references were people I had met in the previous twelve months before applying to the Residency.

As you try to make your own luck and welcome serendipity, know that the possibilities are endless. Things like this can happen:

1. You meet someone who is also reading the same book on the bus or train and make a connection you otherwise would have never talked to.
2. You attend a future event I am speaking at and make connections with like-minded people, and maybe even meet your future best friend or spouse.
3. You have a conversation with someone about something you don't usually think or talk about and the seed is planted for you to explore a new career path, opportunity, or adventure.
4. You make introductions for others, and when you least expect it those connections make fruitful introductions for you.
5. You listen to a song that you've heard a hundred times, only to receive the artist's message differently this time, and fall in love with the artist's style and music.
6. You make a generous gesture of kindness to a total stranger, and that stranger calls you and leaves you a voicemail to say thank you. You keep the voicemail forever because it reminds you of that day and gives you a great feeling each time you hear it.

7. You are rejected from the promotion you always wanted or the job of your dreams, and then find the work you really love.
8. People give you advice, but you choose to go with your heart. You find out someone you admire chose the same path you did, and you pursue it and find joy along the way.
9. You share your stories of serendipity with others who could not previously see how they could welcome the serendipitous moments in their lives.
10. People thank you for your presence in their lives and tell you how it has opened doors for them. This inspires you to welcome serendipity even more.

These are just a few of the myriad of ways we can experience and keep our eyes open for serendipity. When we do, life can become a lot richer, and a lot more fun.

HAVING FAITH IN YOUR STORY

One of the hardest experiences I went through writing this book was wondering when the words I wanted to write were going to come to me. I'm confident in my ability to convey a message verbally. Speaking in front of crowds is more exhilarating than nerve-wracking for me. For a long time, I thought I would have to use the voice-to-text method in order to get my thoughts down on paper. It bothered me that I had such an aversion to writing. I had forgotten how much I loved writing and performing spoken word poetry in high school and college. I thought writing a book was different from writing an email or a short poem. I worried that the ideas would not be constructed effectively, and the book might sap away the emotion I've become known for communicating with. I didn't have enough faith in my story before I started.

Having faith in your story is about living in alignment with what you feel is your purpose in life and fearlessly pursuing your dreams along the way. With my purpose to make a positive impact in the world, one of my dreams was to become an author who touches people's lives with my words. The only thing was, the idea of becoming an author, for many years, was just that—an idea. I thought one day it would be cool to write a book. I thought it would be cool for people to read that book, but the aversion to writing that I constantly experienced was egged on by impostor syndrome. I wondered if people would even want to read a book that I had written.

Then I met Frances Hesselbein in 2015, and the thought that it would be cool to write a book eventually changed into the realization that I must write a book if I wanted to share my ideas and outlook on the world with others. I learned of Frances's quiet way of communicating powerful messages succinctly and effectively. I read her books, which follow a similar short essay format. I thought that if the great Frances Hesselbein could write in this way, perhaps I could choose a similar approach instead of the longer form books I'd grown accustomed to reading. With France's vote of confidence, I was affirmed in my feeling that I would begin to write.

In the fall of 2016, a conversation with one of my best friends about our aspirations triggered me to sit down and begin writing. When I finally looked up from my laptop screen, about an hour had passed and I had a page or two of typed work done. I couldn't remember what I had just written. There were typos and grammatical errors. It was kind of disorganized, but there were some decently constructed thoughts expressed in it. That was all I needed to know that I was on my way.

I began to repeat the same recipe. No distractions or notifications. It was only the computer and me for 60- to 90-minute blocks of time. No worries about typos or grammar. Communicate freely and openly and see what happens. As you can see from the format of this book, my approach aimed to make visible progress by writing a new essay each time I sat down. This helped me to build my confidence on the path to becoming an author, but I wouldn't have been able to continue without having faith in my story.

Over the years, I've met many naysayers. I've compared my resume to other authors, and I struggled in the process of writing this book. Keeping the faith in your story is necessary because in doing anything worthwhile, we will inevitably hit roadblocks, distractions, and feelings of self-doubt. But that's what makes the effort worthwhile. There are some authors who have written over twenty books. All of them had to start with one. As you read this book, I hope that you find yourself in the writing. I hope that you see some of yourself in the stories. I hope you see some of yourself in me. I certainly see parts of me in you. Discovering what's shared between us allows us to empathize, encourage, and support each other in ways that positively push us forward.

How you keep the faith is acknowledging that your struggles are shared with others who have overcome similar challenges. You keep the faith by knowing that your vision and the future you seek, when you are true to yourself, is possible.

THE UNCERTAIN ENTREPRENEURIAL LEAP

I wish I could tell you exactly when to take the leap into entrepreneurship. But I can't. There is no magical formula for discerning when the moment is right to become an entrepreneur—or whether you've got an incredible idea or if the conditions are ripe to bring your product to market.

Entrepreneurs solve problems and create products in various sectors and regions spanning the entire globe. Because of their extraordinary diversity, I'm not going to tell other entrepreneurs' stories—their stories are already out there. The entrepreneurs who inspire you may be visible in your community, online, or in the magazines you read. I encourage you to seek out and discover their stories. Familiarize yourself with the journeys of entrepreneurs who are doing things you hope to do so that you can better understand why some succeed and some fail.

Here, I share some of the heartaches, pains, and concerns I thought through and addressed before I took the leap to becoming an entrepreneur. By no means am I telling everyone to become an entrepreneur. Entrepreneurship is not for everyone. But if you are thinking about it, keep reading.

Taking the leap from a place of uncertainty can be daunting. Lots of different people gave me advice along the way, but it wasn't until I realized that uncertainty is synonymous with possibility that I chose to pursue possibility.

My entrepreneurial itch started in 2006 when I was working with teenage entrepreneurs in Masiphumelele, a black township in South Africa that was formed during the apartheid era. The WorldTeach program I was participating in paired me and fellow volunteers with Uthango Social Investments, a local social enterprise that exposes youths to entrepreneurship by teaching them how to start and run their own community businesses. We were tasked with collaborating with Uthango to design and facilitate their two-week *Snack Sneakers* program, which featured educational classes and an actual candy shop competition for young teens, where the teens would come up with a business name, take out loans from the "bank," and go out to make sales.

Our cohort of volunteers from America ranged in age from eighteen to thirty. As an eighteen-year-old and one of the youngest volunteers, I felt I needed to do something to stand out on a team of seasoned professionals. I went to the Internet café during our first week to research business terms and their definitions. Knowing that our team had plenty of experience and expertise, I thought the most important thing to focus on was making sure we conveyed our ideas effectively so that they would be heard. Reviewing business 101 terms led us to design the educational classes with the students who were new to the topic in mind. It influenced how we taught a topic to a student who had never heard of a terms like "loan," "stock remaining," and "profit." Stripping it down to the basics made it easier for us to connect with the teens.

During the program we acted as actual bankers and wholesalers and allowed the students to buy and sell sweets and chips while teaching them about other facets such as public relations and marketing. We also stressed principles like respect, commitment, punctuality, honesty, self-confidence, persistence, responsibility, and teamwork. The children were initially attracted to the program because money and sweets were involved, but in the end they realized that there was a lot more to entrepreneurship than that. On the last day, I remember my eyes welled up with tears as the students thanked us in song, a sign that the program was appreciated and had been a success.

Masiphumelele, the name of the township, means "we will succeed" in Xhosa, and I was hopeful that our small contribution helped the community in some small way to live up to its name. After seeing the entrepreneurial spirit of the participants firsthand, I realized that I could be an entrepreneur one day myself. I'm so grateful for the seed that experience planted in my mind.

After the trip, I returned to the United States and started thinking about how I could make an impact on the world. This desire is the lens through which I operate in the world. I believe that my work should have an impact and a significant one.

During the two years I was unemployed after college, I got my first taste of entrepreneurship, jumping on board with an education technology startup that sought to increase transparency and communication between school administrators, teachers, students, and parents. The founder, who had already gained traction with the technology, was excited to bring me onboard to consult and recruit more schools as customers. I could see then, as a twenty-two year old, that I had the unique ability of captivating school leaders once I got the chance to get in front of them. Unfortunately, the founder did not follow through on certain promises to me, so I decided to stop working with the company. It was still a great experience and confidence booster. In 2010, I focused on getting a full-time job because I felt that I still lacked the skills and experience to succeed as an entrepreneur.

I accepted a job offer from Bloomberg LP in the fall of 2011, after a long period of interviewing and unemployment. I felt like my life was back on track, but in the back of my mind, I knew I would only stay at the company until I felt ready to take the leap. I didn't have a clue as to what specifically I would do if I left the company, but I knew growing professionally at one of the best organizations in the world would help.

While I was working, I found myself drawn to reading articles about leadership, personal development, psychology, and human capital. Bloomberg is a go-to information platform for the C-Suite, so it was a good excuse to read up on topics that might concern these leaders. Articles on these topics fascinated me and gave me insight into my own experiences as well as the experiences others shared with me. I wanted to learn so much more, so I decided to invest $9,000 in a coaching certification program. It was a private decision that meant I was on my way to whatever was next.

The program provided the basis for my understanding and practice of coaching that I still use today and opened doors to great conversations with people in human resources and diversity & inclusion at Bloomberg. I was invited to participate in an HR led think tank focused on finding, hiring, keeping and nurturing entry-level talent, and it felt great to have my perspective validated by people who got paid to do the work I was most interested in. My independent reading and personal investment in learning additional skills was paying off. With each affirming conversation I had, and each leadership experience I gained from leading awareness of the Black Professional Community affinity group, I built confidence in my ability to succeed independently of the organization. Despite this growth, I still had serious fears about leaving the certainty and security of working at a company with global brand recognition, benefits, and guaranteed pay every two weeks.

In my search for ways to break through my fear, I turned to one of the greatest leaders of personal development, Tony Robbins. I now had the financial means to attend one of his programs; in fact, I brought along my first business partner and one of my sisters to experience it with me. We attended *Unleash the Power Within*, a four-day immersive personal development seminar, which was a transformative experience. I was in awe of Tony Robbins for being a human being who could guide thousands of participants through such an engaging program.

As a part of this particular seminar, participants are given the opportunity to walk across a bed of hot coals, a symbolic gesture that encourages participants to get over any fears they came to the conference with. We each chose to do it and walked away from the experience as firewalkers—people who would never let fear get in our way again. Or so I thought.

Once my sister, business-partner, and I returned to our respective lives in different cities after that peak experience, we each implemented the new strategies we had learned into our lives. While we had all progressed, the biggest fear I had intended to erase was still alive and well. I wanted to quit my job, but feared it would be a mistake. In the ensuing months, I questioned myself for being so afraid. I decided to attend *Unleash the Power Within* a second time with more friends and family a few months later that same year. This time, my intention was to get rid of my fear for good.

During the seminar, participants expend a lot of energy learning how to move instantly into what Tony refers to as "peak states." Having already experienced the program, I saw myself as a role model for the other participants. Even when I was tired, I could still muster up more energy, and that process of building resilience to fatigue, in many ways, is what breaking through your fears is all about. I felt stronger in my mind and stronger in my body about the decision I'd gone to the seminar to make. After crossing the hot coals triumphantly a second time, I knew life would never be the same again. This time I was ready.

I went back to work and while I didn't quit immediately, I knew this time that the clock was ticking. I felt a deep sense of freedom from that point forward, and I began to excel in both my volunteer diversity & inclusion work and my role in sales. The work was more fun knowing that I wasn't looking for the next promotion, and I could focus on building towards a bright, independent future.

Nearly a year later, sitting in an airport in Madrid, Spain, I finally decided I would leave the organization. As I sat there waiting for a flight back to the U.S. after an awesome four-country, seven-city vacation, I couldn't help but think what my life could be like if I were to design it myself. Where could I go? What could I do? How many people could I serve through my work? Instead of scaring the hell out of me this time, these questions excited and inspired me. I knew it was time to begin my speaking and coaching journey of inspiring and uplifting people to reach their potential in college and at work.

Now, you should all know that I embarked on this journey without any existing clients and no certainty of success. Besides my belief in my ability and potential, and my faith that God would guide me along the way, all I really had was a couple thousand dollars in the bank and a dream. As you contemplate your ideas and the decisions ahead of you, I want to share a few lessons I hope will be helpful. Here are my lessons, in no particular order of importance:

- **An idea is not a business and an idea is not perfect when it is first formed.** I held on so tightly to my ideas when I first began thinking about starting a business. Only a select few family members and friends were in the know, and they hardly challenged my ideas. I've since learned that there is no shortage of ideas in the world, but there is, unfortunately, a shortage of people who take action on their ideas. The years since I left the corporate world have been a non-stop learning experience and a period of continued iteration, experimentation, challenges, and refinement. The idea that I started with was just the beginning. It has taken so much more to build a business. Like the stones in a stone shaker getting refined into gems, ideas are often refined into useful products and services for people through a grueling process building, testing, and rebuilding.
- **Failures, big and small, are inevitable.** To succeed as an entrepreneur, I had to shift the meaning of failure in my mind to better serve me. What if I wasn't making money? What if I couldn't share a positive success story with my former

colleagues in a few months? What if potential clients didn't see the value in my services? The facts were: I wasn't making any money, I didn't have much to share with my colleagues, and potential clients were not seeing the value in my services. Had I stopped six months in, I would have never realized that my success was not going to happen overnight. In fact, most "overnight success stories" are preceded by years and years of pouring out blood, sweat, and tears before a person, product, or company finally gets their big break. For me, failure is a flashlight that illuminates an area where I need to grow and learn. Instead of thinking that failure is an indication that I should stop, I thank failure for showing me where to go. Instead of looking backwards and thinking, "Maybe all of the people who thought I shouldn't do this were right," I look forward and think, "How can I approach this differently next time?"

- **You can overcome your fears.** There will always be a voice inside our heads that questions whether we are good enough. On my leadership and entrepreneurship journey, I've dealt with this voice by creating new meanings of experiences based on a few personal statements that I live by. Here are three of them:

1. Every day is an opportunity to learn, grow, and have fun. I am free from the burden of feeling like I must know it all, at all times. I remind myself to have fun and experience joy every day.

2. God has a plan and I'm going to live in accordance with his plan for my life. With my faith in God, I have nothing to fear. I believe He will never give me more than I can handle, and He will reveal his plans for me as He sees fit. All I have to do is show up, do the work, and trust that He will show me the way.
3. Every day is a gift. Beyond the work, I think about all of the incredible people and miraculous things in life I get to experience just by being alive. Some people are grateful for this simple fact only after facing death. I don't think we should wait.

The decision to become an entrepreneur is a personal one. If you decide to take the leap and pursue that path, keep these lessons in mind as you strive to succeed.

YOUR ACTIONS

MANAGING MENTAL HEALTH
THROUGH ADVERSITY

I am thankful that mental health is getting more attention as various influencers and everyday people are speaking up about their own challenges with mental health and the need for us to address the stigma around this issue in society. The stigma around mental health is a problem that keeps too many people suffering in silence. People need to know that there is no reason to feel ashamed about how they may feel or the illness they may be suffering from. Seeking help is not a sign of weakness.

According to the Anxiety and Depression Association of America, anxiety disorders are the most common mental illness in the U.S., affecting 40 million American adults age eighteen and older, or 18.1 percent of the national population every year. That's nearly one in every five people, and much more common than we may think. On a global scale, the World Health Organization reports that depression affects over 300 million people of all ages globally and it is the leading cause of disability in the world.

So here we are, with a chance to shine light on the dark periods of our lives and break free of the weight of suffering. Here, I share one of my stories.

When I graduated from college in 2009, the global recession was still near its peak. It was difficult for students in my class to land jobs. I did not have a job when I graduated, but I was optimistic that I would find one. There were a few things working against me it seemed. I wanted to work at a top company, but I didn't have the highest GPA, and I had no idea what kind of career I wanted to pursue. I was interviewing at great finance companies, but the interviewers could see that I was not genuinely interested.

Fast forward a few months, and I found myself feeling like a failure. I remember asking my sister one day if maybe I should lower my expectations and aspirations for myself. Maybe I was thinking too big and this was a reality check. It was like a big slap in the face that was telling me that while I went to a great college and had some great internship experiences, I was still mediocre at best.

This is how I developed a story that began to harm my mental health and the belief that I could succeed. I was fed up with the job search process and fed up with myself. I knew I had potential, but for some reason I couldn't convince others to believe in me. I spiraled into a dark place, avoiding conversations with friends who were "doing well" or who had jobs and were living the dream in New York City. I was the kid voted "most likely to succeed" in high school, but here I was, seemingly failing at life.

Then, thanks to encouragement from my sister who asked around for help on my behalf, everything started to change. It turned out one of my cousins was familiar with temporary work agencies in New York City and was willing to make a connection for me. I got an interview, passed their qualifications, and landed a paid opportunity! The pay was not that good, but I was grateful to get out of my house, put a few dollars in my pocket, and experience the feeling of progress.

During this time, I discovered my appreciation for personal development as I read lots of books and watched lots of videos from some of my favorite personal development experts of all time, like Jim Rohn, Tony Robbins, and Les Brown. I also stumbled upon the book *Now, Discover Your Strengths* and the StrengthsFinder talent assessment tool that I now am certified to use to develop others' strengths.

In retrospect, I realize that the low self-esteem and lack of self-worth that I experienced is not that much different from so many people who struggle with low confidence and fears that they are not good enough. From that experience, I learned that mental health challenges can affect anybody, no matter how significant or insignificant the cause may seem.

If you are reading this and you feel like your mental health is not where you'd like to be, here are a few things you can do starting today:

1. Know that you are not alone and that you can talk to someone without feeling ashamed. If you harbor the negative feelings and isolate yourself from others, it will hurt even more. Don't be afraid to seek help.
2. Look out for and be grateful for the little things; our fears run away from gratitude. Fill your thoughts each day with gratitude for something you learned, the breath you have for another day, something beautiful that you see, or a nice interaction with someone. The present moment is enough.
3. Know that this time in your life will pass, and you will be better off because of what you struggled through. I firmly believe that these periods in our lives don't just happen to us, they happen for us to prepare us for what lies ahead.

4. Start to change the way you move. As hard as it may be to feel like getting up to do anything, it's worth it to incorporate exercise into your life, even if only for a few minutes a day in the comfort of your own home to start. When you exercise, your body releases more endorphins and serotonin, which are the two main chemicals in our bodies that boost our mood and produce a positive feeling. When we build up our positive feelings, we're likely to have more positive outcomes. I've also encouraged people to dance and be playful when thinking about the obstacles and issues they may be dealing with, to dissociate from the solemn thoughts that can feel like heavy weights on our shoulders. You don't have to be a good dancer to dance, just enjoy a few minutes of playfulness and see what happens.

5. Share your story. TED Speaker Nikki Webber Allen founded an inspiring nonprofit organization called I Live For... to break the stigma around depression, anxiety, and other mental disorders. She hopes that by sharing our stories and facing our issues head on we can reclaim our lives. Our stories can also inspire others to speak up and speak out. Our world needs a movement to stop this global problem. Let your voice be heard.

My personal experience taught me how to be more resilient in the face of adversity. It taught me to have even more appreciation for the people who love me. It led me to discover my love of personal development and this beautiful thing called life, which I am blessed to share with you today.

BEING AUTHENTICALLY YOU

Living with authenticity is hard. We are constantly changing and growing. There are so many influences vying for our time and attention at every turn: from our social and professional circles, to our social media presence and living in the world at large. Every day, people are shaping how we think, what we do, and how we feel about our lives. It's so important to take the time to turn our attention inward, to make sure we are aligned within ourselves, so that we can give the outside world what feels most true from the inside.

That's why I've included the authenticity worksheet that I use with various audiences that I speak with to help you on your journey. The worksheet is located on the last page of this essay. You can duplicate it and use it anytime that you want in your own personal journal or scrap paper.

This worksheet will serve you as an honest guide and exercise for checking in with yourself whenever you need it. It will help you to define what it means for you to excel while also being true to who you are.

What Makes You Come Alive

Right now, I'd like you to think of the last time something you were working on made you feel alive. As you think of it, answer these two questions in the first box of the worksheet:

What were you doing? Why did you feel that way?

Because of our various interests and professional endeavors, the answers to these questions will naturally vary widely from person to person. To jumpstart your thoughts, here are some examples that people have shared with me.

The last time I felt alive I was...

- Organizing an event – because the process of figuring out how all of the moving parts come together is really exciting
- Writing a blog post – because translating my thoughts into a tangible, written form helps me share my thoughts with others
- Presenting the results from a team project – because all of the hard work that we put in led to something we could share and be proud of
- Coaching one of my direct reports – because seeing someone grow as a person through my guidance is really rewarding
- Speaking with one of our customers – because I was receiving feedback directly from the people we serve and I felt energized to help them even more

Take a few moments now to fill in the top of your worksheet.

By identifying what makes you feel alive, it becomes easier to restructure your life so that you can do whatever gives you that feeling time and time again. Whether you're doing the same activity or something similar to it, you know that it's going to give you a specific result—the feeling that you are ALIVE.

If we took this approach to our careers, we could look at job roles and responsibilities and easily determine whether the work would make us feel alive or not. In our current roles, we could make a change to our workflow to include more of what make us feel this way and reduce the work that doesn't. If we are designing our own careers, we can decide how we want to spend our time each day and each week. This is incredibly important in an era when so few people are engaged at work. If each day you could look forward to doing something that makes you come alive, that would do wonders for your engagement at work. By finding greater alignment with the activities that consume your time every day, you will be doing things that feel more true to your authentic self.

Your Need to Fit in & the People Around You

The workplaces we go to, the social circles we're a part of, and the social media platforms we participate on are chock-full of traps to pull us away from our authenticity. In the workplace, one challenge is figuring out how to fit in. In 2013, Kenji Yoshino, the Chief Justice Earl Warren Professor of Constitutional Law at New York University School of Law, and Christie Smith, the former National Managing Principal for the Deloitte University Center for Inclusion, collaborated on important research published in a paper called "Uncovering Talent: A New Model of Inclusion." Their findings are so powerful that I recommend reading the entire paper, but here is a short excerpt that explicitly highlights the challenge of adapting to the workplace:

*In 1963, sociologist Erving Goffman coined the term
"covering" to describe how even individuals with known
stigmatized identities made a "great effort to keep the
stigma from looming large." Goffman gave the example of
how President Franklin Delano Roosevelt ensured he was
always seated behind a table before his Cabinet entered.
President Roosevelt was not hiding his disability—everyone
knew he was in a wheelchair. However, he was covering,
making sure his disability was in the background of the
interaction. In 2006, Kenji Yoshino further developed the
concept of "covering." He elaborated the four axes along
which individuals can cover: Appearance, Affiliation,
Advocacy, and Association. Appearance-based covering
concerns how individuals alter their self-presentation—
including grooming, attire, and mannerisms—to blend into
the mainstream. For instance, a Black woman might
straighten her hair to de-emphasize her race. Affiliation-
based covering concerns how individuals avoid behaviors
widely associated with their identity, often to negate
stereotypes about that identity. A woman might avoid
talking about being a mother because she does not want
her colleagues to think she is less committed to her work.
Advocacy-based covering concerns how much individuals
"stick up for" their group. A veteran might refrain from
challenging a joke about the military, lest she be seen as
overly strident. Association-based covering concerns how
individuals avoid contact with other group members. A gay
person might refrain from bringing his same-sex partner to
a work function so as not to be seen as "too gay."*

Do you cover along any of these axes? If your
answer is yes, you are not alone. According to the research,

the following percentages of participants surveyed reported covering along at least one axis:

61 percent of all participants
83 percent of LGB individuals
79 percent of Blacks
67 percent of women of color
66 percent of women
63 percent of Hispanics
45 percent straight White men

When we cover, we are working two jobs. The first job is consciously monitoring and maintaining an image that may not be true to us, and the second job is the actual job we are paid to do. Covering is a taxing effort that literally drains our authenticity like a faucet with a gaping hole in it.

While much of the onus is on organizations to proactively address employee needs for diversity, inclusion, and belonging, I'm always drawn to what we can do as individuals. When we understand and accept who we are and invest the time to raise our awareness of the parts of our identity that we're not willing to negotiate on with others, we can confidently approach interviews and opportunities with a knowledge and confidence in who we are. Our future depends on this because when we deny ourselves the chance to stand comfortably on our own two feet, we resign ourselves to the status quo. If you've ever covered, or if you know someone who covers, I know you don't believe the status quo is enough. So let's change it. The more honest we are with ourselves, the more honest we can be with others, whether it's in the workplace, our social circles, or through our social media presence.

The next section of the worksheet is meant to help you understand the relationship dynamics of the people who you spend time with, so that you can make some tough and honest decisions that will help you get closer to being who you are and living by your values.

In the middle of the worksheet, you will see a plus sign and a minus sign on opposite sides. I'd like you to imagine for a moment that your life has a numerical value, and the people who you spend time with either add to that value or subtract from it. Life is not a mathematical equation, but if you were to think about the effect people have on you, you can see how this analogy is relevant.

The first part should be fairly easy. On the side with the plus sign, write down the names or initials of people who:

- Celebrate your accomplishments as much as or even more than you do
- Express genuine interest in your well-being
- Make you feel like you are enough
- Are a positive influence on you and encourage good decisions
- Are motivated to become better and also motivate you to be courageous and daring in living your life to the fullest

Now the part that may be a bit harder to write down. On the side with the minus sign, write down the names or initials of people who:

- Dismiss or try to one-up your accomplishments
- Downplay how you're feeling when you feel down
- Make you feel insignificant

- Are a negative influence on you and encourage you to make bad decisions
- Complain about their situation, but never do anything to change it, and don't actually want to see you change your situation either

Hopefully, the list on the plus side is longer than the minus side. If it's not, you've got some work to do and some decisions to make about how and with whom you are sharing your time and life. Ideally, your life will one day overflow with people who are adding to it, with few, if any, people who subtract from it.

Another way you interact with people is through social media, which can become tedious and frustrating to keep up with. When you see people doing things on your bucket list, accomplishing their goals, and generally doing cool stuff, it's important to take note of how you feel. When you see comments, posts, or content that violates your values or attacks you directly, it's important to think before you respond. When you catch yourself posting something just for a like, ask yourself if the likes actually matter. I've found that the following three principles have helped me navigate my social media experience during times when I've been frustrated with it:

- Take a break – when you feel like you need to step away from social media, take a few days off or an entire week. No notifications, no late night peeks. Off.
- Notice comparison, the thief of joy – as tempting as it is to compare what you have to what others have, and what you are doing compared to what others are

doing, feelings of envy and jealousy will steal from your joy.

• Choose respect in conversations – it's no secret that social media conversations often turn into shouting matches, insults, shaming, and unnecessary swearing, with little to no accountability. Part of the reason this happens is the fact that people are communicating with each other from behind a screen, saying things they wouldn't dare say to someone face to face. But if we want to change the conversation, it starts with us. If each of you reading this was to change your approach to how you communicate and respond to people, it would make a big difference. I encourage you to be an example of someone who communicates with respect, kindness, and curiosity.

Your Personal & Professional Brand

On the bottom of the worksheet, you will see a section with the words "personal" and "professional." I'd like you to think of yourself as a walking brand. Every day, you send messages to other people through your appearance, how you conduct yourself, how you work, and how you lead. When you know what your personal and professional brand is, or what you would like it to be, it's easier to consistently live your values.

Think about what you want people to know you for. Fill in the worksheet with the words and phrases that come to mind. Have fun with this exercise. Start with the personal and then move on to the professional. Here are a few examples for both:

64

Personally – a good person, positive, thoughtful, playful, physically fit, open-minded, family oriented, financially smart, loving, stylish

Professionally – ambitious, high standards, delivers on promises, resourceful, insatiably curious, dedicated, passionate, team first, savvy, trustworthy

You can use what you write as guideposts for living authentically. As with any brand, living by your words consistently will be a challenge, but the experiences along the way will only help you grow as a person and as a leader. I encourage you to envision the day when you don't have to constantly think about who you need to be in different parts of your life—when you don't have to shift to be a certain way with one person or group and another way with someone else. Being authentically YOU is being YOU consistently and not settling for anything less than discovering and sharing the best YOU you have to offer.

MY AUTHENTICITY WORKSHEET

The last time I felt alive I was...

(+)

(-)

Personally

Professionally

CHANGING YOUR
NETWORKING APPROACH

Have you recently attended a networking event eager to
collect every business card, meet the person with the
highest-ranking title, or snag a new opportunity from
someone who's attending? Have you ever failed to follow
up with someone you met at an event even though you
promised you would?

For too long, my answer to both questions was yes.
In college and my early twenties, I was an eager networker,
ready to make an impression and rub shoulders with people
with the most senior job titles. My attitude was definitely
influenced by the novelty of networking opportunities,
where I could meet people in this fashion, since I had not
had any exposure to networking before college. I loved the
challenge of getting business cards, and I'd often collect so
many that I was too overwhelmed to send a follow-up
email to each individual I had met.

In most of those scenarios, I was the person who
was looking to get something out of the new relationship
created. I was the college student looking for an internship,
the unemployed person looking for a job. When I got a job
at Bloomberg, I was on the other side of those
conversations, meeting people eager for opportunities to
intern or work at the company. For the first time, I felt like
some people were just trying to use their connection with
me to get a job, and it didn't feel very good. I was
disappointed when people who I had enjoyed meeting
promised to follow up, but didn't. I realized that most

people network the way I used to—showing interest in company names and titles and not keeping promises to stay in touch.

In reality, very few people actually build relationships that last after meeting at networking opportunities, and most people operate in a space of transient transactional connections where it is extremely difficult to genuinely get to know anyone. Once I realized this, I decided that I wanted to stop networking and instead become a person who builds relationships. That decision has served me well and I've since developed dozens of great relationships that have withstood the test of time because I approached building them the right way.

Here are the six principles that guide my approach to networking:

1. **Be Generous.** *The New York Times* bestselling author Adam Grant writes in his book *Give and Take*, "The most meaningful way to succeed is to help others succeed." I've experienced so much joy from helping people find personal and professional success. Whether it's making a quick introduction between two people I think should meet each other or recommending a resource for someone to look into, helping others has been very rewarding. The really neat part is, whenever you do actually need something, people who have benefitted from your help in the past will generally be happy to help you. The key difference between transactional networking connections and these kinds of generosity-based relationships is that your relationships might turn into genuine friendships that last for years, where unexpected opportunities

may arise just because you are in good standing with someone. Your task from here is to start approaching every new person with the mindset of giving instead of taking.

2. **Seek What Excites You.** Conversations are so much more interesting and easy to remember when two people who have never met share a genuine common interest. As you prepare to enter a room with the mindset of building relationships, think about what you are passionate about at the moment, what you'd like to learn, and what topics are really interesting to you. Do yourself a favor by being true to your interests and helping everyone you meet see who you really are. Plus, nobody likes people who are faking interest or wasting their time.

3. **Learn from Everyone.** I believe every person can be both a student and a teacher to you. Stop worrying about what company someone works for or what job title they have. You can learn from anyone and offer value to anyone. When you're open to learning from anyone, you can always gain a new perspective. People have interesting stories and lessons to share from what they have learned through their specific life experiences, past careers, transitions, and following their dreams.

4. **Keep Your Promises.** We all get busy. Life happens. Emails pile up. Friends, family, and children take up our time. It's hard to keep up with everyone you know, much less every new person you meet. One simple thing has worked for me: keeping my promises. If I tell someone I will send them an email or get in touch on social media, I do. It may take a few days, but I follow through.

Keeping your promises means being selective when you say, "I'll reach out so we can meet for coffee," or "I'll introduce you to ____ because you two have to meet." If you make promises to everyone it becomes really hard to keep them. Being thoughtful and selective forces you to really make your follow-ups worth your time and the time of everyone involved.

5. **Welcome People In.** In 1:1 conversations, make the other person feel like they are the most important person in the room. Try your best to avoid wandering eyes, which signals that something more important is happening elsewhere or someone else is more important. Great eye contact and open body language signals that you are present in the conversation and welcomes the person you're speaking with to open up. In situations where you are in a circle of people where there is one person everyone wants to talk to, be kind enough to invite someone else in if they are awkwardly on the outside. Most times, that person will be appreciative that you welcomed them in.

6. **Stop Asking "What do you do?"** It's not uncommon for people to ask "What do you do?" within moments of meeting each other. Maybe you have the habit of asking people this question. It's a poor question to ask because it doesn't help you learn anything meaningful about the person besides their current role or company. They might say, "I'm an accountant at XYZ Company." It's a great question to ask for transactional networking, but if you're aiming to build relationships, it doesn't help much. I've found the best way to disrupt the pattern

of this question is to ask alternative questions and give a nontraditional response to traditional questions.

You could ask these alternative questions:

What brought you here this evening?
How did you get interested in this topic?
What was your favorite part of your day today?
What's something interesting that you're working on right now?

You can start your response to their questions with:

"I woke up this morning excited about..."
"One thing I'm really passionate about is..."
"I'm curious about..."
"A few days ago someone asked me that question and I told them..."

People will probably be surprised when you respond this way, but you will be a lot more memorable than someone who simply says, "I'm a (insert title) at XYZ Company."

I hope that these six principles will serve you well in building lasting relationships that will enrich your life and career.

REKINDLING THE ARTIST WITHIN

When we were children, we could scribble something with a crayon or draw stick figures and proudly call it art. Our parents and teachers might have said, "Wow, look at that!" This kind of positive response is both a celebration of the child who is learning new skills and encouragement to continue creating. At that tender age when it doesn't matter what you put down on the paper, everyone sees you as an artist.

For some reason, as we grow older, whether it is school grades or society's influence, we start to view our art as imperfect or substandard, and sometimes not as art at all. We look at the Van Goghs and the Picassos of the world and think to ourselves that there's no way we are artists. We forget the beauty of how we used to be—the times when we could freely put pen, marker, crayon, or brush to canvas to create and celebrate without judgment.

Can you remember the last time you felt this kind of freedom with your art? Was it sitting with a paintbrush in front of a canvas, or was it through your voice, writing, or dance movements?

As a teenager, I used to read Bible selections aloud as a lector in my church. When I was in college, I wrote and performed spoken word poetry in front of my classmates. Since then I have spoken professionally in front of many audiences. I frequently get compliments on how I use my language, articulate, and uniquely express my views and ideas clearly and with emotion. Public speaking is my artistic gift and I generously share it with every audience I get in front of, so that they may see the world differently after listening to me. But selfishly, public speaking also allows me to feel like I'm "the zone."

If you have ever been in "the zone" or heard of a star athlete describe being in the zone, that's kind of what being in flow feels like. It's a moment in time when you are absolutely locked into what you are doing and you are doing it with ease and excellence. Many times I have done speaking engagements and noticed that I can't remember exactly what I said because I was in flow. It's as if the words and language pour out effortlessly. When I started to experience flow with my writing, I realized simultaneously that working on my voice and writing at the same time had enhanced both practices.

As my mentor, Frances, likes to say, "Communication is not saying something; communication is being heard." When we are too judgmental about our form of expression, we lose our ability to enjoy ourselves and the process of creating. Judgment confines us into boxes where we think we can only create things one way, as opposed to creating with freedom and expressing what feels true to ourselves.

With nearly 8 billion people in the world, someone will be ready to appreciate your true expression, so it's really up to you to decide what your canvas will be and how you want to share your art. Whether it will be for personal joy or to share with the masses, and whether you sing, dance, write, compose, speak, draw, design, or paint, someone will be glad that you decided to rekindle the artist within.

FINDING YOUR WHY & YOUR CAUSE

I usually don't think too much about death because I love living so much, but recently a new acquaintance asked me a question that made me think about it. "So tell me," she said, "who is Torin Perez?" In that moment, I replied, "Here lies a man who lived every day with a purpose and made a positive impact in our world. If I decide to be buried when I die, I would like my headstone to be inscribed with this message."

In stories I've heard from people who have encountered near-death experiences, the feeling of being given a second chance can give us a deeper appreciation for life, allowing us to live more fully each day. With Father time being undefeated, I believe it's so important for us not to wait until we are on our deathbeds or have a near-death experience to begin to live, love, and experience life at its fullest.

As we meet people in our lives and we are asked what we do or what we're passionate about, we can all too easily pigeonhole ourselves into the box of our current occupation or title. We can even attempt desperately to connect our career decisions in a logical order, though we know our path may look more like an unpredictable web and crisscrossed lines.

After reading Simon Sinek's book, *Start With Why,* and watching his TED Talk many years ago, I was inspired to think about finding my own WHY. The why is about having something to live for so that we can find purpose and fulfillment every day, and this is exactly what I sought to do. I wanted to help other people navigate to this point as well, and through many conversations I've learned that the challenge is figuring out how to do this in our current world of work.

According to the Gallup State of the Global Workplace 2017 report, only 15 percent of the global workforce feels engaged at work. Similarly, the Gallup State of the American Workplace 2017 report revealed that only 33 percent of the American workforce feels engaged. In the U.S., the independent workforce consisting of freelancers, contractors, and temporary employees is expected to grow to more than 40 percent of the general workforce by 2020. Whichever part of the workforce we occupy, we still seek to live fulfilling work lives, and we must consider changing our approach to successfully do so.

We could argue that most companies and their leaders are not doing a great job of helping workers find this fulfillment. We could also argue that most of the people who seek to work at these companies do not cultivate enough self-awareness to know what they truly want. We must begin to invest even more in ourselves to discover what we care about, what drives us, and what's important to us. Only then will we be more thoughtful in our approach to employment and seek work that we can truly give our time, energy, and spirit to.

I'm fortunate to frequently meet people who think deeply about their lives and how they would like to live each day. These people are some of the happiest people I know because they take time to identify and dedicate themselves to work they love. I can honestly say that I love doing just about anything that makes a positive impact in the world and I love to see other people committed to doing work that they feel affects people in a positive way. It could be the social sector leader who is serving the community. It could be the person who is using technology to improve our quality of life. It could be the CEO who is absolutely committed to making sure every single employee feels safe at work and fulfilled from what they do. Most of the time we feel we must select one specific path, but we should be flexible and open to change. Out of a single WHY we can set ourselves up to contribute to many causes in multiple ways.

Setting my WHY to make a positive impact in the world has freed me to imagine the myriad of possibilities that are available to do so. I speak and consult with companies looking to address workplace inclusion and leadership development. I have given guidance and coaching to leaders, such as my peers preparing to do TED Talks in the TED Residency program, an incubator for breakthrough ideas. As an advisor to DreamAfrica, I support an organization on a mission to celebrate cultural representation and inspire cultural understanding.

Over the years, I have paid close attention to my journey, from childhood to the present, looking back in hindsight to see connections and thinking in the moment about how I feel about what I'm doing. With this approach I have gained the freedom to diverge from certain roles in pursuit of other paths. I believe this approach allows us to observe how we feel about the work we're doing with honesty, to discern which changes are necessary to help us live out our WHY.

It's important to be aware of how you're feeling on a daily basis so that you are in tune with your internal compass. When you are in tune with yourself, instead of walking away from a job the moment things get tough, you can ask yourself, "Is it worth it to stick with it?" When you are living out your WHY, a clear sense of purpose makes it easier to say, "Yes," and overcome the challenge. So the key is to consciously look at your life and deciphering it as you go.

You must seek out the people, programs, and experiences that can provide clarity on what you want to be doing with your life. With technology, it's a lot easier to reach out to people you admire, and people who truly serve causes are always looking for help. You can write a thoughtful email or make a phone call to an organization you want to support or be a part of. You can reach out and ask someone to have coffee. As you look to hone your skills, don't hesitate to invest in continued learning, certifications, and events that will enrich all that you can give. Many of the world's best colleges and universities offer free online courses in 21st century skills. The opportunities are boundless once you decide to identify your why and live through your causes while applying your skills. You no longer have to continue asking yourself about your WHY in some head-in-the-clouds kind of way. Just get started. Think about the words you want your headstone to be inscribed with. Chances are, if you even live up to half of the description, you will have certainly made your mark and led a life worth living.

OWNING YOUR WORTH
THROUGH FAILURE

How would your life be different if you learned how to fail gratefully?

I define "failing gratefully" as being grateful for what your failures help you to later do or become.

Every time we fail, perceive we have failed, or are told that we have failed, our core human need to feel like we are enough is threatened. Whether you are failing to stay standing on a pair of skis, to excel at your job, to maintain your intimate relationship, or to raise your children the way you envisioned, failure stings.

The sting of failure is something we never really get accustomed to and can last for minutes, days, years, or a lifetime. For some of us, the pain grows so great that we hide and remove ourselves from what we were doing entirely. Too many of us are hurting in silence because we're ashamed of our failures and shortcomings. But what good is it to be silent, when your voice can help others break their silence?

I started to understand the gravity of failure in our lives when I met a janitor who was cleaning the trash at an event I had attended for small business owners in Brooklyn. I acknowledged him and thanked him for cleaning the place up. He was wheeling a cart with a trash bin and cleaning materials when he paused and pointed at the cart saying, "This. This is not what I ever dreamed I would be doing.

Eight years ago, I had a job, a great job in finance, my own office and everything. I was doing well, taking care of my kids and my family, and then I got laid off. Twenty-seven years I was at the company, and they laid me off. I never quite recovered from that and I gave up on corporate work. So I do this a few times a week. It's okay. I try not to feel embarrassed when I'm around my kids because their dad is a janitor."

Every day this man lives in pain. Getting laid off completely uprooted his sense of self-worth and he never recovered from it. In his mind, his failure to keep his job meant he failed himself and his family, and life has never been the same since. I wonder how his life may have been different if he failed gratefully. He could have looked at the layoff as just one door closing to make way for another door opening to something even better—a lifestyle where he could happily spend more time with his children or an opportunity to reinvent himself in pursuit of a new career path deserving of his talent and experience. I can only imagine what his life might have been had he chosen to interpret what happened to him differently.

If we want to become the best versions of ourselves and the leaders the world needs, then we must subscribe to the philosophy that we own our worth, even when we fail.

At the TED office in New York City, there is a poster on one of the walls that reads: "Make no small plans." Indeed, it is precisely our big plans and dreams that give us the reason to strive through the trials and inevitable failures we will face along the way. It is the inevitable failures, both large and small, that make a life with big plans worth living. Anyone who makes small plans will surely achieve them. Small plans are small because they are safe. But without challenge, there is no growth, and without

80

growth, we die. So how safe is it to play it small, really? This is why we must make big plans.

So what might failing gratefully look like in your life?

Would you receive a poor performance review and use it as motivation to become the best people leader you could be? Would you use a layoff at a job you hate as the reason to start the company you've always wanted to run? Would you take the decline letter from the school on your wish list as a sign that a better school experience awaits you somewhere else? Would you use the insights from a failed product launch or business to try again with a more informed strategy? Would you acknowledge that you have no idea how to parent because it's your first time, allowing yourself to seek advice and help from others?

While it's true that over the last four years I have facilitated learning and development sessions and spoken to over fifty colleges, conferences, organizations, and Fortune 500 companies, I have failed many times. I have had a few experiences where my audience seemed disinterested and gave me poor reviews. I have made what I thought was a great pitch, only to lose out on opportunities to other competitors. While questioning my product pricing time and time again in attempts to make it easy for companies to decide to work with me, I've ended up selling myself short, later learning what they would have paid. But it is because of these internal battles and external disappointments that I've become who I am today. I thrive and I succeed because of these failures.

I own my worth through failure and I do everything I can to fail gratefully, absorbing and re-channeling the blows of defeat into new energy and passion for the journey, knowing that I'm better now because of it.

I don't know what your plans are or what you're dealing with in life, but what I do know is that we are a very resilient species. What may feel like your greatest failure today, may be the door opening to your greatest success tomorrow. And with a philosophy like that—that no matter what you do, you will fail gratefully—you will be ready to walk through the door of success when it opens.

CHOOSING YOUR
FELLOW TRAVELERS

The first woman to be featured on the cover of
Businessweek magazine and a recipient of the Presidential
Medal of Freedom for pioneering work for women,
diversity, and opportunity, Frances Hesselbein is an
extraordinary person who I am lucky to call a dear friend.
When we first met she told me that we were fellow
travelers: people going on the journey of life together. Our
journey constantly reminds me of this quote from Dr.
Martin Luther King, Jr.: "Those who love peace must learn
how to organize as effectively as those who love war." The
message is so succinct, yet powerful, and I've lived by that
statement since the first time I saw it. The premise is
simple: if you want there to be more good in the world,
take action to help the people who are making it better.

Frances is a paragon of what Dr. King was talking
about. She is always excited to hear from leaders from all
walks of life, offering her wisdom and stories to support
them along their way. She understands the importance of
uplifting those of us who love goodness, and I also
understand the importance of this through first-hand
experience. Through various communities I'm a part of,
including StartingBloc and the TED Residency, I've seen
the power of sharing resources, building partnerships, and
supporting one another wholeheartedly. It's clear that the
impact that we make on each other personally and the
impact we help each other create through our work

wouldn't be possible if we were on our own. In these programs, participants become fellow travelers.

While most of us may not have the good fortune of joining communities like this, in our travels and in our day-to-day lives, there are people we end up spending a lot of time with who form our personal community. It's so important to pay attention to the people who surround us and walk with us on our journey.

In some small way, I share the stories in this book so that I can be a fellow traveler with you. There may be people like me who you keep at arm's reach on your bookshelf, and people who you follow online who you may never meet, but it's the people you spend the most time with who will have the greatest impact on the direction of your life.

I was disappointed when I learned of personal development icon Jim Rohn's passing. Since I first discovered him in 2010, I had always wanted to meet him because the wisdom from his talks and seminars on YouTube impacted me so much. His words still touch me, but it's been the actions I've taken because of his words and the people whom I've taken action with that has made the biggest difference in helping me become who I am.

As you take stock of your closest friends, family, colleagues, mentors, and role models, think carefully about what they bring to your life, and what you bring to them. Are they good influences on you? Do they make you want to become better? Do they genuinely celebrate your progress and successes? Do you feel like you are growing together? Do they share information and resources that help you? Do they tell you they believe in you and your potential?

On the flip side, are they bad influences on you? Do they seem to be envious or indifferent to your achievements? Do they seem completely fine with complacency? Do they love to engage in gossip? Do they frequently complain? These are just some of the questions you can use to gauge who your fellow travelers are and should be.

In grade school, we may have had a certain group of friends. Perhaps we made new friends in college, at work, during our travels, and while exploring our interests. At every stage you should be thinking, do I have the right people around me? If you are married and your friends are constantly talking about how they will never get married and how many people they know cheat all of the time, they might not be good fellow travelers. Perhaps you may be better off with people who do want to get married or who are already married and thriving. If you're succeeding financially in your career and your friends only invite you out to treat them, they probably aren't your real friends. If your role model is a social media star whom you have never met, make sure to stop and think about the fact that many people are selective with what they post and describe publicly. These days it's easy to create a profile with beautifully curated pictures and videos, but that may only tell one side of the story. Don't get caught up in the hype, and remember to live your life, not someone else's.

As you look for mentors, seek people who are a few steps ahead of where you are in your life and career, and make sure they are good at listening to you and teaching what they've learned. If you have a mentor, you should know that it's possible to outgrow a mentor. Someone who is an appropriate mentor to you while you are in college may not be able to mentor you when you are building your own company. A person who was very successful in a particular field may not be able to mentor you in a different field. Things change and people change, and as we grow we must choose when to hold on and when to let go. And it won't necessarily be easy.

I'm not telling you to dump your childhood friend who has been there for you since you were in diapers. But if they are not a positive influence in your life anymore, and you are trying to grow into a better person, you may want to limit the time you spend with them or encourage them to get with the program you're on. We can pull our friends ahead with us if they want to come; we just can't let them pull us back.

As you move forward and achieve success, there may also be new people who try to get on the bandwagon. Beware of people like this, who never cared who you were before your success and will leave just as quickly as they came if you fail. Beware of the people who come into your life because of your money, fame, lifestyle, or material wealth. When there is nothing else to take or get, they will leave.

Make it a priority to think carefully about the people you bring with you on your path. Over the years, the faces may change, but the goal remains the same; to continue striving and thriving in the game we call life. As you select the players on your winning team, think about whether they will practice hard, stick with you through the adversity of losing seasons, and celebrate your successes as much as you celebrate theirs. Those people will be the best fellow travelers.

PRACTICING THE RARE
ART OF LISTENING

When I was a little boy, an older basketball teammate of mine named Lucas bullied me for a few weeks. I always wondered what drove him to threaten to take my stuff and eat my food. He would tell me if I ever told my dad about what he was doing there would be consequences. I feared him. But when I finally got over the fear of speaking up, I told my dad about everything Lucas was doing, and my dad verbally reprimanded his actions.

What always stuck with me from that exchange was observing how my dad communicated to make Lucas change his ways. He was stern and clear when he pointed his finger towards Lucas and said, "Don't you ever even think of messing with Torin again, or else you will never step foot in my car again." "Messing" may have actually been another word, probably an expletive for emphasis, but it was too long ago to remember. What I do remember was that Lucas listened like his life depended on it, and after that single encounter with my dad, Lucas never attempted to bully me again.

Because of this experience in my early childhood, I've always been curious about why people think and behave the way they do. Often I find the answer to this question by listening.

While I was working at Bloomberg, I spent a lot of time in the office snack pantries having conversations with old friends and making new ones. I looked forward to every snack break I took because I couldn't wait to see what conversations I might have each day. Some conversations with coworkers were about how we'd spent the weekend. Some conversations were about interesting projects and deadlines we had to meet. Some conversations were about getting to know the other person, taking 5 minutes here and 10 minutes there, to exchange personal stories and build our friendship. Some conversations were about our careers and some were about tough times. Although I enjoyed all of these conversations, I especially enjoyed the ones where I felt the pull to help a person get through a challenge. I was often asked for advice, but sometimes I was just asked to listen.

I remember working late one evening because I was buried in a project due the following day. It was probably 8 p.m. already, and I thought everyone on my floor had long left the office when I heard a cough. I looked behind me and saw my colleague Mathias working intensely at his computer, headphones in and eyes glued to the screen.[1] The next time I took a break I asked him to join me so we could empathize with each other's situations. While we were talking about what we were working on, I could tell that he was worried about not being able to complete his project in time. As I inquired about when his project was due and how long he thought it would take to complete it, he told me he might have to stay overnight. I told him I thought that was ridiculous. He replied, "Honestly, I feel like they're always doing this to me. There's always too much work to be done, and I'm always the one who has to stay and do it. It sucks man, and I think if I don't get this done in time, I might get fired."

---

[1] I have changed the names of some of the people in this essay to protect their identities.

Mathias didn't know that I was in the middle of a coaching certification program and that I was taking every opportunity I could to practice the coaching skills we were building. Around that time, we were practicing the art of listening—the ability to discern what people are saying and what they're not saying. Though we were cordial with one another, this was our first extended conversation, and Mathias had just told me he was scared he might lose his job. I felt pulled to help him in that moment, and luckily, I had just acquired the skills that would allow me to do so, so I put my coaching hat on to see if I could help. I started by acknowledging and validating his feelings about the situation, which had an immediate effect on him. It seemed he hadn't felt heard in a while and just voicing his feelings to someone who was genuinely listening brought relief.

I saw a physical shift in his body as his shoulders moved from being slumped to straight. When I asked if maybe he was going a bit far in thinking he could be fired, especially since he had been doing his job well since we both started working at the company, I saw an emotional shift in him. He agreed he might have been being a little too hard on himself. I suggested that he was probably more appreciated than he thought and that one of the reasons he was getting stuck with the work was because they trusted that he was the right person to get it done.

After our short conversation, Mathias returned to his desk with a content smile on his face. I left the office shortly thereafter when my work was done and looked forward to seeing him the next morning. When we had a chance to catch up the next day, he told me that he left the office shortly after I did. Instead of staying late, he came into the office early to complete the project. He finished it in time and said two simple words to me, "Thank you."

I credit listening to him as part of the reason why he succeeded.

Over the years, I've helped people navigate difficult situations like this, make career decisions, prepare for job interviews, and get ready to do TED Talks. The one thing that makes the biggest difference in reaching each person effectively and helping them the way they need to be helped, is listening to each of them as if they are the most important person in the room and listening for what they're saying with their words, vocal tones, and bodies.

The late great Peter Drucker, known as the father of modern management, once said, "The most important thing in communication is hearing what isn't said."

As a leader, if you want to communicate effectively with individuals, there is no better way to do so than to start with a foundation of listening. Listening is easy to practice, yet so many people rarely do it. In individual conversations, take notice of how many times you interrupt other people mid-sentence, zone out when you're supposed to be listening, or forget what someone just told you. During group conversations, take notice of how frequently you are the first to speak. When you become committed to developing your listening skills, the frequency of these occurrences will be limited, and you will find yourself becoming a better listener. But really, the fun begins when you realize how well you listen helps the people around you—when they know you truly hear them, they can tell you what they really mean.

LEADING ACROSS DIFFERENCE

Companies around the world are trying to figure out what it means to lead across difference. With spotlights on the challenges people face because of their gender, race, religion, age, disability, and sexuality, viral news stories and social media documentation can ruin the reputations of brands that display ignorance, indifference, or tone-deaf responses to these protected classes. As just one example, we've seen technology companies in Silicon Valley go great lengths to publicly display demographic data and make investments in talent pipelines to avoid further public backlash for their lack of diligence in the recruitment and retention of diverse talent.

While most companies will focus their diversity efforts on expanding their recruitment pools to bring in more people from underrepresented groups, research has shown that diversity, without inclusion can actually hurt company performance. The prioritization of inclusion must go hand-in-hand with the focus on increasing workforce diversity, which means the active and consistent practice of building safety and demonstrating the behaviors that welcome diversity. When done right, inclusion is one of the big reasons why companies retain diverse talent and keep that talent engaged at a high level. In particularly tough situations, like the aftermath of the shootings of Alton Sterling and Philando Castile in 2016, leaders and companies that made compassionate public responses to the tragedies received positive recognition for speaking up and offering support to any employees having a difficult time.

Companies that responded poorly or didn't respond at all were looked at as indifferent, insensitive, and even dangerous for not tending to the needs of black employees and all employees in general who were saddened, outraged, and disturbed by the video-recorded tragedies.

The pain we experience as humans is something we all share and that I believe is the foundational thread for leading across difference. Oftentimes we don't feel like our sadness, anger, or pain is processed the same way someone else's sadness, anger or pain is, yet we are biologically wired to process these feelings in the same parts of our brains. In 2003, social psychologist Naomi Eisenberger shared some fascinating findings in her research paper titled, *"Does Rejection Hurt? An fMRI Study of Social Exclusion."* In a simulated virtual ball-tossing game in which participants were ultimately excluded, fMRI scans revealed increased activity in the anterior cingulate cortex: the same part of the brain that lights up when we feel physical pain. While the types of exclusion we may experience in our lives may be different, the way our brains interpret it means that each of us are hurting when we feel excluded—and people who are hurting may also be harming morale, customer relationships, and themselves.

I share this because when we do make the effort to build inclusion consistently, great things can happen. Inclusion is not just about taking the unconscious bias training your company offers or reading the latest research paper. It has a lot to do with how you show up every day in conversations with your colleagues, and what you ask for and fight for on a regular basis. It's speaking up even when you feel like someone else will if you don't. It's contributing wherever and however you can to build inclusiveness and safety at your company, even though the demands of your day-to-day work may leave you with little more to give. It's focusing on the people who are delivering the results, not just the results themselves.

During my time at Bloomberg LP from 2011 to 2013, I remember feeling the sting of exclusion because I often felt I was on the outside of some of the cliques that existed on my team. I wasn't interested in getting my shoes shined every day or buying overpriced custom suits, and this made me crave an outlet to be with people who shared my values. In early 2013, I heard about some new initiatives at the company to start Employee Resource Groups (ERGs), which they decided to refer to as communities. I jumped at the chance to be a part of it, and the executives leading the Black Professional Community (BPC) appreciated my energy and fresh face as a fairly recent hire.

In the fall of 2013, the BPC was getting ready to put on an important event. Since Bloomberg was fairly new to the ERG space, our goal was to make a loud statement about the value we brought to the firm and our efforts to build a safe and inclusive company culture that would benefit all employees and clients alike. For months, we had planned a program focused on the business case for diversity. We had been able to get a well-known head of diversity & inclusion as well as our head of human resources to sit down together for a discussion that would enlighten the leaders from our firm and employees from other organization ERGs in attendance. The program was a success, which was an important moment of validation for the mere existence of the community.

Looking back, there is much to be proud of in my work with the BPC. In just fifteen months, I spearheaded community membership growth and raised it by more than

150 percent as co-chair of the awareness committee. The heads of diversity and inclusion and philanthropy recognized what I contributed through both internal engagements and programs to uplift non-profit partners like Harlem Educational Activities Fund (HEAF). These were visible and tangible wins that made a difference during my time at the firm, but they are not in and of themselves what I am most proud of.

What I loved the most, and what I am most proud of to this day, is the openness to exchange that we advocated for and created at the firm. I loved being a part of these communities and the chance to have informal conversations with people who I may not have otherwise met. While I understood that the main focus of my volunteer leadership role was to serve the interests of the BPC, I also understood that getting the buy-in of people outside of our community would be critical to our success.

Being who I am, I made lots of friends and acquaintances while at the company, both as an intern in 2007 and 2008, and when I returned full-time in 2011. Coffee breaks or meetings in the snack pantry were always welcome opportunities for people to stop and say hello or have a brief conversation. As my work in the organization began to pick up with my role in the BPC, I imagined bringing all of my friends and acquaintances into the fold. At the very least, they could volunteer, attend an event, or tell one of their colleagues about us. I was always thinking about how we could engage more people beyond black employees and members of the BPC.

I believe movements should be inclusive, and my thought process was influenced by one historical event in particular. At Dr. Martin Luther King, Jr.'s *I Have a Dream Speech*, a quarter of the people who attended were white. I didn't believe women's community programs should only have women in attendance. I didn't believe any of the communities should have only members of that community attend. When I looked at our membership, the vast majority of members were people who identify as black, but we also had members who identified across the spectrum of diversity. We had different kinds of faces in the audience at our programs, all brought together to advance the goals of building a more diverse and inclusive environment where everyone can succeed and thrive.

During my time as a part of the BPC, some seasoned employees whose growth had been halted at the firm began to see doors open for promotions, new responsibilities, and new opportunities. These were some of the fruits of making the effort to lead across difference. I was also proud to be a young person at the firm with the ears of senior leaders. My ideas were always welcomed, and thoughts were always exchanged respectfully. It was beautiful to see senior leaders build connection and understanding with me and other young employees. Our open exchange is an example of what's possible in managerial relationships, where managers may think the young employees are entitled and the young employees think their managers don't want them to get promoted faster than they did. Great work relationships are possible through mutual respect, managing expectations, and communication.

There were still barriers to our efforts as some managers had antiquated thinking about what makes meritocracy work and didn't understand the need to support and acknowledge certain communities in the first place. We didn't view these barriers as a sign to turn back or tune down our efforts, but rather as opportunities to involve, inform, and inspire new ways of thinking. The spirit of active and consistent work towards inclusion is the magic in the wand we want to wave to make the world better. Change never happens overnight, and we should know that. Change is created through constant and challenging work, engaging believers, and winning over new champions. Bringing about change is a fulfilling journey that has the power to energize and help us lead from where we are, across any differences that may exist.

FINDING THE HEART
OF REPRESENTATION

Asingia and Franco, the co-founders of DreamAfrica, were classmates of mine at Lafayette College. We were all a part of the International Students Association (ISA) and took part each year in the organization's annual event *Extravaganza!* The program featured students cooking and sharing food from different regions of the world, and the finale was a show that featured dance, music, and performances by students representing different countries. It was an experience we looked forward to every year because it allowed everyone to feel seen and valued for the uniqueness that they brought to the campus community.

I had no idea that our shared experiences at ISA would later lead us to work together on DreamAfrica, which came into existence because we felt that the diversity of African stories were not being told in mainstream media. Everywhere we looked, stories about Africa were told as stories of poverty, war, and disease. There were few if any positive stories, like *Lion King*, *Black Panther*, and *Bino & Fino*. When I agreed to join the organization as the global product evangelist, my role was to publicize the fact that the company existed to celebrate African stories from diverse voices.

In early 2016, Franco and I took a couple of trips to Nairobi, Kenya, to hire new team members and set up our Africa office operations. One of the most memorable moments of the trip was seeing how news of what we were working on touched a local Kenyan woman. As we explained to her how she could record her grandmother telling stories in kiswahili on our digital platform, she couldn't believe that we were serious. With watery eyes, she told us how much it meant to her that we were willing to help preserve her heritage. She felt seen on a deep level.

That moment, along with many others, shaped how DreamAfrica (now known as DreamGalaxy), has become an advocate for change and inclusion in the multimedia storytelling industry. The organization has been featured on stages from TED to Harvard to accelerate awareness of our initiative. Once solely focused on breaking apart the idea of a monolithic African culture, creatives and brands from dozens of countries in Africa and around the world have joined us, aligned with one common belief: people and their stories matter.

We all know what it's like to feel invisible. Perhaps you've been the last person to get picked for a team, been left off of an invitation list, or felt silenced and unacknowledged in a professional setting. If getting picked sooner, receiving an invitation, or feeling welcomed and included in a professional setting is what it means to be seen, representation serves a similar purpose. When representation is at its best, there is a constant effort to ensure differences are welcomed, appreciated, understood, and shared.

Thankfully, representation is starting to take up a more prominent space in the minds of influential people. Conference organizers that get it right choose not to have homogeneous speaker line-ups. In the tech industry, the *50/50 Pledge* initiative works to showcase gender balance across the voices at the top technology industry conferences. With companies taking heat publicly for tone-deaf advertising, the need for representation in marketing decision-making is obvious. So many of the problems that arise in marketing to a diverse audience could be mitigated by having a diverse team helping to create marketing campaigns in the first place.

Companies need to understand that people want to see themselves and feel like they can be a part of what the company is doing. Some airlines use greetings in multiple languages in their welcome aboard videos and cast people from a wide range of demographics. When done right, I've found these efforts meaningful because customers who fly around the world are as diverse as they come and they will feel a connection to the airline because they saw someone who knew their language or was from the region they are from. This is so important because the customers onboard, just like the customers in any industry, could be spending their money elsewhere. People want to see themselves and know they are seen, and marketing with a focus on representation is one great way to help people do that.

As a Posse Scholar during college, I organized on-campus events that brought people together from different corners of campus. Whether it was spoken word events, student and staff discussions, or social events, I wanted to see people from fraternities and sororities, sports teams, Posse, and the general student body coming together. Organizations I was a part of did this exceptionally well, and we were recognized with various awards for our leadership on campus. But I wasn't the only person who had this perspective. The people on the leadership team and the organizational body were all recruiters, and we made sure we had representation from all of the groups that we wanted to take part in our events. It made it so much easier to enroll the participation of Greek Life members because a member of Greek Life led one of the organizations I was a part of. Athletes, who typically kept to athletic circles, attended certain programs because some of our organizers were athletes. And the list goes on.

When I meet students on college campuses who say, "Free food and drinks aren't enough to get people to come out," I share what I believe the real key to success is: representation. If you are organizing an event and you want attendees from different groups or diverse backgrounds to attend, just take a look at your organizing committee, your volunteers, and past attendees. If the demographics are homogeneous, you can rest assured it will be difficult to achieve your goal. So the solution for new event organizers is to recruit and include a demographically representative organizing team from the start. The solution for existing organizational leaders is to address gaps in representation so you can start to include more people now.

We know men make up the vast majority of chief executive officer roles in corporations. There are actually so few women CEOs in the S&P 1500, that there are more CEOs named John than women. The companies that will stand out in the future are the ones recognizing that the gender imbalance and lack of diversity must change now. From corporate boards to the C-Suite, countless studies have highlighted the value of diversity in leadership, but where it really matters is in the hearts and minds of your workforce.

When your employees look at your leadership, can they see themselves? Do they feel limited in how high they can rise or how far they can advance? Part of what leads to high turnover and failed recruitment efforts is failing to address these limitations and not making a commitment to change.

On *The David Rubenstein Show: Peer to Peer Conversations*, Oprah shared the following perspective about what she sees as the common thread in all people around the world:

> *What we all want, is to be able to live out the truest, highest expression of ourselves as human beings.*

When we find the heart of representation, we not only encourage people to reach for their highest potential, we take action to help people get there.

YOUR IMPACT

RAYS OF SUNSHINE

Living an inspired life is about seeing the rays of sunshine that illuminate the dark human challenges and experiences that we face in our world. In 2016, I was fortunate to take part in the inaugural class of the TED Residency program. The residency offered residents the chance to incubate ideas in a collaborative community with twenty-seven leaders from different disciplines. My fellow residents were highly intelligent, generous, humble, ambitious, caring, and dedicated to their chosen paths. The fourteen-week program allowed each of us to hone in on a specific project and define how we are making our mark on the world— daring greatly, sacrificing much, and not letting go of ideas we believe are worth spreading. The residency culminated with each of us delivering six-minute TED Talks in New York City.

I felt deeply humbled and privileged to work alongside people who are just as motivated as I am to aspire and excel in their chosen craft. The residents in my class worked on a diverse and dizzying range of projects, including utilizing live storytelling events to catalyze restorative and transformative approaches to ending mass incarceration, promoting violence prevention for at-risk, inner-city youth, creating visual media to demystify complex scientific concepts, lobbying for policy changes to save the ocean, inspiring youth of color to pursue engineering careers, and challenging the fashion industry to rethink inclusive design. Each entrepreneur, artist, scientist, and activist provided daily inspiration for me because of the positivity and optimism they maintained while trying to solve some of the most complex and pressing problems of our time.

Living in an era when the future of our world can feel grim, all I had to do to improve my state of mind was look to my fellow residents who were brightening the way.

According to TED, "An idea worth spreading doesn't just magically appear out of thin air. Instead, it needs a long incubation period, a sometimes frustrating—and often exciting—trial and error of creation, failure and innovation." Despite being spread across the spectrum of diversity and achievement, we all identified with the frustrations and excitement of learning by trial and error. The results of any incubation period are often unpredictable with no guarantees of success. The precarious nature of living in uncertainty can feel daunting, especially when your finances, livelihood, and general wellbeing are at stake. All of us residents wondered at some point if we should give up on our projects because of a roadblock or problem, yet at the same time, we racked our brains trying to exhaust all options to find a way to make things work.

Before joining the TED Residency, I thought people like this, with never-say-die attitudes, were flat out crazy. But after joining the program I realized I was crazy too. You see, sometimes you find something that lights you up, inspires your emotions, and beckons you forward to take an action. Consciously, you know that the odds may be stacked against you—failure is more likely than success—but your heart is a powerful force. Your unconscious mind will help you find the answers when your conscious mind cannot. Your heart will welcome people in so that you can move the mountain together. When our brains say no, our hearts say YES!

On July 12th, 2016, our class took the stage to deliver TED Talks on each of our projects. That evening was a time to be grateful for the opportunity to share our ideas with the world. It was a time to acknowledge the legacy of the TED brand and all the speakers who had graced the stage before us. It was a special honor to become a part of that legacy on that day.

I've since met dozens of residents who have become part of the semiannual program, and each class carries a torch illuminating the world around us. While the program only takes place in New York, I'm encouraged by the fact that residents have traveled from far and wide to take part. Their participation is a reminder that people who are committed to making positive contributions to the world are everywhere.

If you look hard enough you will find people and organizations online and in your community working towards positive change. Keep looking until you find the stories, causes, and leaders who inspire you. Just remember that each of them started somewhere. Your story is still being written, and it might just be your ray of sunshine that we're waiting for to light up the world.

THE LEGACY YOU LEAVE BEHIND

Tony Robbins once said, "What we give is what we keep, and what we fail to give is the only thing we lose in this life." As we age, and as we search for meaning in our lives, the desire to leave a legacy grows. We start to think about what we will leave behind to our children, our friends, our family, our community, and our world. We start to ask questions like: How will I know that I made an impact while I was here? How will I know my life was worth something to someone else? However, living in order to leave a legacy may not be the best approach to successfully building one.

There are so many variables in life that we have no control over. Think about it: we have no control over what people will write or say about us when we're gone. We have no idea how other people's ideas or interpretations of our lives will influence the perceptions of others. Without any guarantees of how people will look at our lives long after we're gone, what we can do is give our all to this moment right now.

I think about the people who surround me, people working for causes and serving missions that are likely to outlive them. Is it possible to clean up the world's litter, save the ocean, or end homelessness in one lifetime? Maybe, but like I said, there are no guarantees. People who aim for success in the corporate world have no guarantees that the company they work for will continue to succeed after they leave or even continue to exist. That doesn't mean we shouldn't try to achieve and give as much as we can.

And what about people who aim to be the best parents they can be? In most cases, our children will outlive us and we won't get to see how their lives continue to change and develop. All we can do is give our all to them in this moment right now.

Think about the words I quoted from Tony Robbins. What we fail to give is the only thing we lose in this life. When the dreams, ideas, creations, and inventions inside our heads are never realized, they're lost forever when we pass on.

But, you may ask, how can we keep something that we've already given away? Well, think about it. Think back to the last time you gave someone a gift and it really gave you a good feeling inside. Maybe it was the person's smile, their hug, their thank you, or the impact of your gift on the person's life. You kept that good feeling, right?

There's a reason why the holidays are meant to be a cheery time of year. Before the craze of shopping took hold, gift-giving was about generosity and kindness, both emotions that catalyze the happy chemicals in our bodies. Similarly, there is a tangible benefit to the exchange of good feelings that comes with happy customers, transformed lives, and solved problems. What we give is what we keep.

Someone I think will leave behind a tremendous legacy based on her positive impact in the world is Debbie Bial, the president and founder of The Posse Foundation. Posse started because Debbie once met a student who told her he never would have dropped out of college if he had his posse, or crew of friends and peers, with him. Nearly thirty years later, and over one billion dollars in college scholarships awarded, the Posse Foundation now stands as one of the premier organizations encouraging and supporting students to pursue a college education. There are thousands of inner-city youth, just like me, who became Posse Scholars, attended top colleges on full-tuition scholarships, graduated because of the support of our posses, and progressed to successful careers. Posse Scholars have touched dozens of college campuses, workplaces, and communities around the world. The far-reaching impact of the Posse program is truly immeasurable. So the question becomes, how does it add up? How do you measure the legacy of a program like Posse?

The truth is, you can add data points to just about anything, but perhaps the real measure is the impact you make on another person's life, and how the work you do makes people feel about themselves. Perhaps it's the ripple effect of you helping someone and that person helping someone else.

The truth is, we have no way to know what our legacies will be once we're gone. But while we're here, we certainly have a say. And it's not so much about what we say, as much as it is about what we do. You might be known as the woman who always found a way to make people smile, the man who was always kind and thoughtful, the person who chose selfless leadership over self-interest, the person who paid it forward to bring other people along with them on the journey to success. We don't have to give away millions of dollars to leave a legacy. Every day, we can do something that adds to our living legacy by using our gifts to give something meaningful to others. And that contribution is worth leaving behind.

INCLUSIVE LEADERS
OF THE FUTURE

In the near future, I envision a growing number of people will begin to stand out from the pack and become the leaders we need for one simple reason: our times demand it. It's known that building a company to thrive with diversity is a business imperative for companies that don't want to get left behind in the past. But who are the companies and inclusive leaders who will move us forward into the future?

      I'm looking at Generation Z growing up today and they will be exposed to diversity in a way that older generations could never dream of. The U.S. Census Bureau predicts that by 2044, there will be a new multicultural majority in the United States. And even sooner, by 2020, half of the nation's children will be part of this new majority. The ubiquity of social media and the Internet will continue to connect people from across the globe and expose people to places and experiences they never would have had access to before. Generation Z will have so many more opportunities to forge connections with people across differences.

      How will these young leaders think about the world when they are in the workforce? A young leader with a different perspective might suggest marketing to a previously underserved demographic that has big buying power; however, their intrinsic motivation for making that proposal will look a bit different. When you have grown up being exposed to people who come from different backgrounds, cultures, and beliefs and exhibit values of openness, kindness, compassion, and respect from an early age, the result is an intrinsic desire to connect with others. In this environment, you are drawn to others with a curiosity to discover, learn, connect, and build trust. The leaders of tomorrow will be less concerned with surviving than they are with trying to serve customers with diverse needs and backgrounds. How the next generation does business and makes decisions will be inherently different than today's business leaders.

Today, many of us wonder why it's so hard to change people's hearts and minds when we see discrimination against people from different social, economic, racial, and cultural groups. Inclusion and cultural sensitivity is too often top of mind only when it's convenient. I believe the leaders of the future who are going to stand out from the rest are not the ones who'll be thinking about cultural sensitivity. They will be the ones who have simply grown up with it in their DNA, leading with innate cultural intelligence.

I'm optimistic about the leaders of the future because of people who I've met through organizations like One Young World. At the One Young World Summit, young talent from global and national companies, NGOs, universities, and other forward-thinking organizations join world leaders to address pressing world issues. These young leaders, between eighteen and thirty years old, are selected from 196 countries. Leaders like Kofi Annan, Mohammed Yunus, and Paul Polman attend the annual summit to address these young leaders with a focus on tackling the Global Goals for Sustainable Development.

As an ambassador at the 2015 summit in Bangkok, Thailand, it was inspiring to meet leaders who have big hearts and lofty aspirations for making positive change in companies and communities around the globe. Diversity & inclusion have only become corporate buzzwords in recent decades, but for the generation behind us, their exposure to diversity will be all they know. Think about the fact that I was in my twenties the first time I saw an iPad and learned how to use it. Now children intuitively know how to play on these devices as soon as they begin practicing their motor skills.

What I dream of is a world where intrinsically-motivated, inclusive leaders will make up the vast majority of leaders in the world. I believe Generation Z is the generation that will make this a reality, but I also believe hope is not lost for us in older generations. The optimist in me believes there is hope for all of us. I'd like to offer three actionable ideas to elevate your leadership starting today:

1. **Live with respect for all.** Respect the janitor, the CEO, the formerly incarcerated. Regardless of rank or role, every human life is valuable. Fill up your well of positive regard for others by having respect for all from the start.
2. **Challenge yourself to interact frequently with people who may be different than you.** They might be different in culture, perspective, language, race, religion, interests, education, socio-economic status, or professional industry, just to name a few. This could be through networking, travel, reading, varying your learning outlets, or anything outside of a homogeneous routine.
3. **Practice bringing a spirit of curiosity to your interactions with others.** Ask questions without judgment. Seek to understand. Listen first. Speak

last. By doing this, you give yourself the opportunity to walk away from every interaction richer than you were walking into the exchange through more authentic connection, stories, and understanding. Perhaps you will open the door to new friendships that wouldn't have been possible with a spirit of close-mindedness.

The future grows brighter with each step we take toward greater understanding. By taking a few small steps daily, you too can become an inclusive leader of the future.

SEEING YOURSELF LIFE SIZE

One day a mid-career woman approached me after a seminar I facilitated and told me how she was losing hope in her aspirations to become an executive at her organization. Since the start of her career, she had aspired to one day become an executive at a company. Over the past few years, though, she had not received a significant promotion, and the feeling of stagnation left her feeling dispirited and unmotivated about her potential to achieve her dream. While I listened and offered her some encouragement to keep going, the wise advice I wish I could have shared with her in that moment came to me a few months later.

Seeing yourself life size is a concept I learned about in a conversation with Frances Hesselbein, who has written about this concept in her book *Hesselbein on Leadership*. When I told Frances about the mid-career woman, she shook her head and said, "That's a shame. She is not seeing herself life size." Seeing yourself life size is about seeing yourself as a whole human being, no less and no more than anyone else. When you see yourself life size, you recognize that each day presents an opportunity to be someone who contributes to the people and situations around you.

The woman I talked to was missing this important perspective. The stalling of her career had shifted her focus to a cynical view of the future, and instead she was focused on the likelihood of failing to reach her goal. If this woman was seeing herself life size, she could have thought about the other ambitious women in her organization who are also striving and young girls who may have similar dreams twenty years from now when they are all grown up. Instead, she shifted the focus to herself, magnifying her perceived inadequacies for promotion, and distancing herself from a positive outlook on her life.

My conversation with Frances made me think about all of the women of the past who fought and paved the way so that the women of the present could have social and professional opportunities. Many of these women had no idea whether they would live to see the fruit of their actions. They did not know if they would live to see women gain the vote or witness another woman run for President of the United States. They didn't know if they would see the day when gender equality was achieved, but they knew by trying they would help others get closer to getting there in the future. This is what seeing yourself life size is all about. It's knowing that your contributions matter.

If the woman had taken this perspective, how might she have approached her career differently? Instead of focusing on herself, she might have seen the larger picture of her organization's goals. She might have thought about whether the organization is promoting policies that ensure women have opportunities to take on leadership and executive roles. Were other women progressing to become senior leaders and executives? If not, how could she have become an advocate, ally, or agent of change? How could she have consistently brought a positive attitude and a winning approach to the goals of the organization? When we realize that our efforts are inextricably linked to the people who follow us, we realize that we are capable of shaping the future ahead for all of us.

As a leader, professional, citizen, and individual, I hope you always remember to see yourself life size. On the occasions where you may forget, use these prompts to get yourself back on track:

> Am I seeing myself life size right now?
> What change do I want to see in my life? And in my world? (Career, personal, family/parental, community, civic, etc.)
> What would I do if I were seeing myself life size?

The world needs you to show up fully every day. Your contributions matter. It's just a matter of perspective.

INFLUENCING YOUNG MINDS

When I was invited to give the opening keynote at a high school Diversity Awareness Week in Connecticut, I was excited to share my ideas with the students. Little did I know that the organizer had made a big deal out of getting me to come speak and on the day of the program, droves of students began to pile into the school auditorium. We were expecting maybe 150 students, but more than 600 students showed up for the session. I was impressed that so many young minds showed up, ready to learn about what it means to become inclusive leaders.

The turnout was a testament to the commitment the school has to developing its students into leaders. In fact, the school has a beautifully written pledge that they hope all of the students and staff members live by:

We, the students and staff of this high school, promise to build a community that promotes mutual respect. We will celebrate our differences and not let them divide us. We will work to understand, educate, and listen to each other.

Their pledge is certainly an inspiring piece of text, but like the Constitution of the United States, any text can remain merely a piece of text unless it is acted upon and lived out. So I sought to challenge and dissect the school pledge, sentence by sentence, bringing the audience's attention to the fact that despite our best intentions, we can still fail to uphold our ideals and values.

I realize that as positive and optimistic as I am, it's also important to remind ourselves of the harsh realities that can come with being human and living with other humans. By nature, we assess new information and stimuli quickly. We naturally build social circles around ourselves that keep perceived threats and differences out, and this sometimes has detrimental effects on our ability to build relationships with new people.

While I typically address professional audiences with this kind of information and insight to challenge and uproot how they think about human differences, I knew that exposing these students to this idea early on could influence them to start to see things differently sooner. I talked to them about similarity attraction bias by showing them how good it feels to find someone you have something in common with. I taught them about social identity theory by observing how each grade level voluntarily sat with their respective grade-level classmates in the lunchroom. Sometimes all we need is awareness to start making changes.

As we imagine who we want to become, we can begin to make changes to cultivate ourselves into that vision. As we grow wiser along the way, we must pay our knowledge forward. I say wiser, rather than older, because an increase in age does not always correlate with an increase in wisdom. If we're wiser in college, we can offer counsel to students in high school. If we're wiser as professionals, we can offer counsel to college students.

I believe our willingness to reach back and share our stories and advice with young minds from elementary school up through college can make ripples of difference in their lives. After I finished my speech at the high school, several people came up to me to let me know that when the students were walking out on their way to the yellow buses, they were talking about what I had shared.

As you think about how you can influence the young minds around you, I'd like to offer some ideas:

1. Expect that a young person may not immediately understand the advice you give. Remember that you had to gain wisdom over time and through experience. Don't give up on them.
2. Expose them to positive things you come across like books, videos, movies, and youth development programs. Make sure the information you feed young people nourishes their minds.
3. Show up. When you get invited to speak on a panel or to share your experience in front of youths, answer the call. It doesn't matter if you're not a professional speaker. This isn't about you. It's about them, and they can learn from you because you're in a place they've never been.

The way we nurture young people today will influence who they become in the future. Let's not miss the critical opportunity to play active roles in their development.

THE BYSTANDER'S OPPORTUNITY

"These are the good Samaritans who helped her," the police officer explained to the EMS team as he pointed to a group of us sitting with the woman who had fallen on the escalator. The date was March 1, 2017, and I was on my way back to New York from a three-day business trip where I had traveled to four cities in three states. I was exhausted, especially after having fought off a stomach bug the night before, and ready to get home and crash in my bed. That's when the incident on the escalator happened, and I felt I had no choice but to take action. It was scary.

In New York City, there are so many things going on and so many people everywhere that it's easy not to pay much attention to all the stimuli: subway performers, the person yelling, teenagers playing, or people sleeping on the train platforms. If you've been to New York City and taken public transportation, chances are you've seen some peculiar and entertaining things. Needless to say, in the city that never sleeps, people are always in a rush to be someplace, even if it's the bar after work for happy hour. Many people are in their own world when they ride the trains—absorbed in a book, wearing oversized headphones, or fading in and out of a nap. These are all the excuses someone might have for being a bystander to a serious situation on any given day, at any given time.

On this particular evening, I had taken New Jersey Transit to Penn Station and I was dreaming about being home when I heard something tumble lightly on the escalator behind me. A tall teenage boy in front of me

125

looked back and then turned back around, a signal to me that it was probably nothing serious. The next thing I heard was a much bigger and louder tumble on the escalator. Then someone behind us shouted, "Can someone up there please help?!"

There were a few people standing between me and the person who had shouted for help, so when I reached the top of the escalator and looked back, I was shocked by what I saw. All of the people behind me continued on their way once they reached the top, revealing an elderly woman riding up the escalator practically on her back! There were two people hunched over trying to hold her up as she came up the escalator feet first, shoes halfway off, with her luggage bag alongside her and her walking cane resting across her body.

I knew we had to do something to help quickly. I looked over to the teenage boy and said, "Hey, I'm going to need your help." I tossed off my book bag and put my luggage to the side. I told him I would grab the luggage and try to grab her immediately after. I grabbed the luggage and threw it to him with my right hand, then grabbed the cane with my left hand and with just enough time bent down to wrap my right arm around this woman to turn her body off of the escalator. We did it just in time.

Those of us who had stopped what we were doing to help were all very thankful for how fortunate the situation turned out. The woman suffered from dizziness and shortness of breath and traumatic events like falling on an escalator can be deadly for a person with that kind of condition.

After we pressed the emergency stop button, I asked the teenager to sit on the ground behind the woman to support her back while we waited for help to come. I learned her name was Ms. Jones, and I told her everything would be okay and that help was on the way. Shortly thereafter, an MTA worker showed up, then a police officer, then EMS. Once the officer showed up, the young man asked if he could leave because he had someplace to be at 7 p.m. We thanked him because he had sacrificed his time to help total strangers when he could have easily walked away.

I stayed with Ms. Jones until EMS took her out of the station. As I put my book bag back on to walk away from the scene, the MTA worker said to me, "Man, thank you for doing what you did. Not many people would have stopped to do that. And I want to thank you personally, because if that was my mother or my grandmother, I would've wanted someone to help."

In that moment I was reminded that one act of generosity can inspire another. When we make the decision to stop being a bystander, we can have such an incredible impact on the people who witness our actions—not to mention the person we're actually helping. There will be many situations that arise where you may think to yourself, *Someone else is going to take action.* Today I want to challenge and encourage you to be that someone.

If you look at the way movements take off, it always starts when individuals come together for a common cause. People speak up, call out what is wrong or unjust, voice their concerns, and walk their talk by doing what they believe is right to create the change they want to see.

The more we decide not to be bystanders, the more we can inspire a culture with a bias towards action where people do not stand by idly and watch. Inaction may be more comfortable and convenient because it's easier to just

127

mind our own business. It's easier not to sacrifice our time and in some cases it may be safer not to take action. But imagine a world where your mother or your grandmother may one day need help, and instead of worrying that nobody will stop to help them, it will be a given for other people to heed the call.

PEOPLE MATTER:
AN IDEA FOR CEOs

In the early 1960s, the United States was in pursuit of the moonshot to land a man on the moon. On one trip to NASA, President John F. Kennedy walked by a janitor cleaning the corridors of the building and stopped to ask what he was doing. The janitor responded, "I'm helping put a man on the moon."

The United States was successful in the moonshot mission when Neil Armstrong and Buzz Aldrin became the first people to step foot on the moon on July 20, 1969. While that historical moment has been remembered as NASA's crowning achievement, it was preceded by years of extraordinary work. In the movie *Hidden Figures*, we learned the story of three important African-American women: Katherine G. Johnson, Dorothy Vaughan, and Mary Jackson—mathematicians at NASA whose discoveries were critical to the first successful space orbit in 1962. For decades, their story went untold.

Countless people contributed to the moonshot mission with a feeling that they were serving a purpose much greater than themselves. In the case of the janitor, he was not just cleaning the corridors; he was creating a clean, ideal environment so that the scientists could be at their best.

I frequently tell this anecdote about JFK and the moonshot janitor because it powerfully illustrates how much everybody matters. Every person who was a part of the team at NASA, regardless of gender, race, role or other differences, came together for one common purpose. We each know how important it is to feel valued. When our work doesn't seem to count towards anything, the hours we spend there feel meaningless, and meaningless work doesn't contribute towards a meaningful life.

As a leader at your company, you must recognize this. Take the time to imagine what your organization could be if you brought the best out of everyone. If everybody feels that they matter, and everybody is working towards a common goal, what's the feeling in the workspace? What are people doing? How do people speak with one another? How do people engage in meetings? What kind of progress is made each day and each week? What are people saying about the company to you? What are they saying when they leave at the end of the day?

As a CEO with high-level priorities, you might be distant from the day-to-day action. You may feel you never have enough time to acknowledge and appreciate your people. You may feel like you don't have time to listen to individual stories. But being a CEO is not an easy job, and your people need you to do the work that is difficult. If you want to build an organization that achieves the ambitious goals you set out for it, you must first exemplify the same values that you hope others will demonstrate. If you want busy managers to find time for frequent one-on-one conversations or check-ins with their teams, they will be more inclined to do so when they observe your example. If you want your people to care about each other and your customers, they will follow your examples of caring for them.

When Frances Hesselbein took over as CEO of the Girl Scouts in 1976, the organization was struggling to remain at its esteemed perch. Frances had observed that the organization would not successfully change course under her leadership unless the organization began to understand the importance and necessity of engaging girls of all cultural backgrounds. Leading an organization with the mission to help every girl reach her own highest potential, she wanted every girl, ranging from an Alaskan Eskimo girl to a black girl in Bedford Stuyvesant, to find themselves in the organization's program and marketing materials. Once girls joined the organization, Frances wanted them to know upon arrival that they would indeed be supported to reach their own highest potential, and they would feel as welcome and special as every Girl Scout who had ever been served by the organization.

During Frances's leadership from 1976 to 1990, the organization's membership and number of adult volunteers grew to record numbers. Thanks to her commitment to reaching all girls, she also tripled the number of scouts from underrepresented racial and ethnic minority groups— a feat that Frances will always be remembered for.

We can build companies where everybody feels included and that they matter when we put people first, as Frances's story shows. When we take care of our people, our people take care of our customers, and our customers add to the bottom line. People who spend 40 hours a week or more in a job or career that they find meaningful are ultimately healthier and happier and contribute more at work. These people are also parents, siblings, spouses, and community members who are better people when they are healthier and happier. When we take care of our people, we take care of our companies, our communities, and our society. As you build your company, never stop envisioning what your company could be at its best, and never stop working to make it a reality.

IN THE SERVICE OF OTHERS

I define leadership as becoming your best in the service of others. Imagine what the world would be like if we really cared about each other. One positive action a day done by billions of people could create exponential positive change. As much as human beings are capable of doing things that destroy, tear down, hurt, and deceive others, we are equally capable of building, uplifting, healing, and genuinely supporting each other. I say this because my life experiences and the people I have encountered consistently provide evidence that deepens my optimism about our ability to build towards a brighter future. I have seen and spent time with thousands of people who are torchlights in the darkness of cynicism. These people give me hope. They constantly renew my faith in our individual capacities to be leaders and they have informed my philosophy about leadership, which I will share with you today:

1. **People from all walks of life can become a leader.** Leaders do not come from a certain place or have a particular background. Leaders realize that ranks and titles may give them power and influence, but titles alone do not make them leaders. At any given moment, our words, actions, and beliefs can shape the way someone else sees, experiences, and lives in the world. Acknowledging this means that we have the power to affect others. With this power comes the responsibility to use it wisely. I honestly didn't realize how much we take our influence on others

133

for granted until I attended various leadership development programs. Even if we may not be good or great leaders yet, we still have the capacity to grow as leaders. I've seen this potential in StartingBloc Fellows, who are accepted to attend a 5-day institute that convenes leaders committed to an equitable, collaborative, thriving world. Fellows are people who seek community, support, and strategies for starting new projects, making transitions, or rekindling the fire in their careers. Some fellows have already embraced the fact that they are leaders. Others emerge with a new lens for viewing their work and the contributions they can make, regardless of their industry or current skill set. Hailing from over 50 countries and all sectors, these fellows have shown me that ordinary people can become leaders when they see a path to starting their own initiatives or leading positive shifts within existing organizations.

2. **Leadership is a journey, not a destination.**
   Leadership is becoming your best in the service of others. I intentionally use the word "becoming" in my definition of leadership because I believe we are all works in progress. Each day is an opportunity to grow more, learn more, and do more in our lives, careers, and communities. Life is not meant to be a linear path that leads to a final place with a sign that reads, "You've made it." While wonderful to celebrate and appreciate, coveted accolades should serve as a reminder of what you still have left to contribute in your life. Remember that age is irrelevant; it's what you do with your life that

matters. You can continue to reinvent yourself and evolve to live a more fulfilled, inspired, and joyous life. This means it's okay to have multiple careers and make transitions. It's okay to come out of retirement to become a first-time entrepreneur. It's okay to learn something from someone who you never thought could teach you anything. In fact, it's more than okay; it's expected of you as a leader. Before I went to South Africa in 2006 as a volunteer teacher, I wanted to be a physical therapist. I've since had experiences in media, finance, hospitality, technology, coaching, learning and development, and leadership. These experiences have shaped who I've become, and the journey will continue to unfold, full of opportunities and possibilities.

3. **Your best self will inevitably serve others.** Is it possible to become rich, influential, and powerful without putting others first? Yes. Is it possible to not be penalized for greed and selfishness? Yes. Is it possible to be respected and admired for identifying as self-made? Yes. The fact that each of these questions can be answered with yes reveals a dichotomy that must be addressed. There are scores of corrupt presidents in countries around the world and scores of corrupt people in positions of power. There are scores of CEOs who care more about their own wallets than their people. I urge you to invest in yourself, cultivating strong character, finding your moral compass, and learning how to empathize with others. You cannot lead others until you first learn how to lead yourself. Your best self is not one overcome with greed. Your best self is

not someone who turns a blind eye to the injustices happening around you. Your best self will not sacrifice your people so you may gain. Your best self will not put others down so you may win. Your best self will know that capitalism affords us the opportunity to build wealth, take care of our families, and enjoy certain privileges in life, but you'll also realize the need to pay forward your knowledge and contribute to good causes. Your best self will speak up or take action to use your influence and resources to contribute to a fair and just world. Your best self will think of ways to take care of your people, not take advantage of them. Your best self will seek out win-win alternatives, knowing that in the long run, progress for many is better than progress for a few.

As we grow, gain skills, and realize our talents, it is possible to attain riches and power without putting others first. I argue today that those who do so are not the leaders we need. We need leaders who are becoming their best in the service of others. We need people like you to lead.

FINAL THOUGHTS

I thought about writing down a long list of the most pressing problems that need to be solved in the world, but the Global Goals for Sustainable Development already outline each problem and the actions required to solve them very clearly.[2] As citizens of the world, we have a responsibility to join in the mission of making measurable progress on these goals by 2030. If you're looking for ways to contribute, spend some time learning about these goals and consider how your strengths might help accelerate them.

I also thought about writing down reasons why you should commit to leading your organization for the advancement of diversity and inclusion in the workplace and society, but the CEO Action for Diversity & Inclusion initiative is already the largest CEO-driven business campaign committed to doing this.[3] The initiative encourages the collaborative sharing of both successful and unsuccessful practices, which contributes to advancing solutions and showing everyone within organizations how to get involved and take action.

So instead of the long list of problems or the reasons to commit to leading, I want to leave you with this poem I wrote:

---

[2] "The Global Goals for Sustainable Development," Project Everyone, accessed March 27, 2018, https://www.globalgoals.org.
[3] "CEO Action for Diversity & Inclusion," CEO Action for Diversity & Inclusion, accessed March 27, 2018, https://www.ceoaction.com.

Why the World Is Waiting for You

The world needs better leaders
It's true and that's all
The world needs us to step up
With acts big and small

Whenever you doubt yourself
And you don't want to believe
Remember we only have one life
So dare to dream and achieve

Don't let your passions wane
Once they are awoken inside
Life is an amazing journey
Passionate leaders serve as guides

So look around close
See the problems that stir you
Write your part of the story
Because the world is waiting for you

ACKNOWLEDGMENTS

On November 30, 2017, I welcomed TJ, my first-born son into the world. As I thought about his life and the wonderful person that I hope he will become, he inspired me to write a book that hopefully withstands time and will still be relevant when he's old enough to read it. TJ, I hope that you become all that you dream to be. Daddy loves you. This book also could not have been published at this time if it were not for his beautiful mother, my wife, Joelle. Joelle, you did everything you could to give me the space and time to complete the book on a grueling schedule. Your words of encouragement and adamant stance that I could meet the aggressive deadlines we set were a big part of the reason the dream to publish this book became reality. I love you for always making me a better man.

To my loving and supportive parents and family, I'd like to express my love and heartfelt thanks. Mom and Dad, you have no idea just how much your encouragement has meant to me in the pursuit of my professional aspirations. Even when I didn't have a dollar to show for all of the effort I was putting in, you stuck by my side like you always have since the time you told me that I could be anything I wanted to be in life. Donica, Shani, Tricia, Amanda, JonJon, Melo, and Ty—I couldn't ask for a better family support system of unconditional love. My heart always warms at the sight of you.

I'd also like to thank several TED Residency community members for being there when I reached out to ask for their guidance and help on this project. Cyndi

Stivers and Katrina Conanan, thank you for telling me that I wasn't crazy to think I could finish the book in less than 60 days before releasing it at the women's conference. Reggie Black, the designer of the book cover and the artist behind #AreYouUsingYourVoice, you produced a cover with the WOW-factor that makes everyone excited to read this book. Thank you for your unique ability to bring the objectives of the cover design to life with remarkable taste and creativity. Katie Salisbury, thanks to your copyediting and developmental feedback, the writing in this book became what it needed to be before publication. Thank you for your keen eye for re-structuring sentences to create the best flow and impact, and for your few but meaningful words of validation. I feel like I grew up into an author during our time working together.

To the Posse Foundation, thank you for betting on me and selecting me for a full-tuition scholarship to attend Lafayette College. The experiences and people I met there have altered the course of my life forever.

To my brothers and sisters in the TTMU family and my Day1s, I'm so happy we have remained so close all these years. Thank you all for giving me a life with so many unforgettable moments. I love you.

Made in the USA
Middletown, DE
05 October 2023

40146546R00090